American
Heart
Association.

D0753788

STUDENT WORKBOOK

HEARTSAVER® PEDIATRIC

FIRST AID | CPR | AED

© 2021 American Heart Association
ISBN 978-1-61669-825-6
Printed in the United States of America

First American Heart Association Printing February 2021
10 9 8 7 6 5 4 3

i

Acknowledgments

The American Heart Association thanks the following people for their contributions to the development of this manual: Gustavo E. Flores, MD, NRP, FP-C; Eric Goralnick, MD, MS; and the AHA Heartsaver Project Team.

Contact Us

Contact the American Heart Association if you want more information on first aid, CPR, or AED training. You can visit **cpr.heart.org** or call 1-877-AHA-4CPR (877-242-4277) to find a class near you.

 To find out about any updates or corrections to this text, visit **heart.org/courseupdates**.

Contents

Part 3: Injury and Environmental Emergencies

"I have someone in my arms who is dying."

Kurt's Story
Survivor's Story

It was early in my shift at the café, around 8:45 on a Monday morning, and I was still feeling tired and groggy. A customer ran up to the counter and asked, "Does anyone know CPR?" A man had collapsed outside, on the patio.

Suddenly, I was wide awake.

I didn't have formal training in cardiopulmonary resuscitation—that's CPR—but I had learned some skills from the American Heart Association website and from Boy Scouts, when I was a kid. At first, I was nervous, but there was no time to waste—somebody needed help now.

Outside, the adrenaline kicked in like a shot of espresso, and I knew exactly what to do. The customer had collapsed in a patio chair. I'll never forget his face—it was as pale as a piece of paper. He wasn't breathing, moving, or responding.

While someone called 9-1-1, we lowered the man to the patio. I remember thinking, "I have someone in my arms who is dying." Another barista held the man's head, and I started CPR. I put both hands on the center of his chest and just started pushing, hard and fast. I kept doing chest compressions and breaths for about 2 minutes, until medical help arrived.

After medical help took over, I washed up, tied my apron on, and went back to serving coffee. But for the rest of my shift, I wondered how that customer was doing.

Later, I found out he was a 66-year-old man named Mike. He survived his cardiac arrest and is doing well. I also found out that most people who witness a cardiac arrest either don't know CPR or are afraid to do it. So, they call 9-1-1—and then they wait. Medical help gets there as fast as they can, but in the United States, it still takes an average of 4 to 10 minutes for them to reach someone in cardiac arrest. The problem is, when someone's heart stops, death occurs within 10 minutes. That means receiving CPR from a bystander is a person's only chance to survive until medical help arrives. It also means any CPR is better than no CPR.

My career goal is to become an emergency medical technician and do search and rescue. But you don't have to be a medical professional to help save a life. By learning CPR, you too can be ready to help someone in cardiac arrest. It might even be a friend or a family member whose life is in your hands.

On your next coffee break, why not take the time to learn CPR?

What You Will Learn in This Course

Welcome to the Heartsaver® Pediatric First Aid CPR AED Course. During this course, you will gain knowledge and skills that may help save a life. You'll learn the basics of how to provide first aid for children (including first aid for the most common life-threatening emergencies), how to recognize a first aid situation, and how to help. You will also learn how to recognize when a child needs cardiopulmonary resuscitation (CPR), how to call for help, and how to give CPR and use an automated external defibrillator (AED).

An important goal of this course is to teach you to act in emergency situations. Sometimes, people don't act because they're afraid of doing the wrong thing. Recognizing that something is wrong and getting help on the way by phoning 9-1-1 are the most important things you can do.

Heartsaver Knowledge and Skills

To respond to a first aid emergency, you'll need both knowledge and skills:

- *Knowledge* is what you need to know, such as what to do if a child has swallowed a poison.
- *Skills* are what you need to do, such as controlling bleeding or performing high-quality CPR.

Your student workbook contains all the information that you need to be able to understand and perform lifesaving CPR and first aid skills correctly. During the course, you'll practice certain skills and get valuable coaching from your instructor.

The video in the course will cover many, but not all, of the skills discussed in this workbook. So it's important to study your workbook to be fully prepared to help in an emergency.

Successful Course Completion

During the course, you'll practice and demonstrate important skills. As you read and study this workbook, pay particular attention to these skills.

If you complete all course requirements and demonstrate the skills correctly, you'll receive a course completion card. Your course completion card is valid for 2 years.

How to Use the Student Workbook

Take time to read and study the student workbook carefully. You should use this workbook before, during, and after the course.

- Before the course:
  - Read and study the workbook.
  - Look at the step-by-step instructions, skills summaries, and pictures.
  - Take notes.

- Review your employer's policies and procedures that apply to first aid. For example, if you work in a childcare center, review what you should do in a first aid emergency. Know how to get help, whom to contact, and steps for follow-up.
  - Make a list of questions to ask your instructor.
- During the course:
  - Refer to the workbook during the video demonstrations and hands-on practice.
- After the course:
  - Review the step-by-step instructions, skills summaries, and pictures.
  - Keep your workbook readily available for reference during emergencies.

Review your student workbook and digital reference guide often to recall important skills.

Learning Objectives

This course includes information about first aid, CPR, and AED use. Course objectives may vary on the basis of the course topics taught. At the end of the course, you will be able to do the following to help in an emergency:

- List the duties, roles, and responsibilities of a first aid rescuer
- Describe the 4 key steps in pediatric first aid: prevent, protect, assess, and act
- Remove protective gloves (skill students will demonstrate)
- Find the problem (skill students will demonstrate)
- Describe the assessment and first aid actions for the following life-threatening conditions: difficulty breathing, choking, severe bleeding, and shock
- Control bleeding and bandaging (skills students will demonstrate)
- Use an epinephrine pen (skill students will demonstrate)
- Recognize elements of common illnesses and injuries
- Describe how to find information on preventing illness and injury
- Describe the risks of smoking and vaping and the benefits of a healthy lifestyle
- Describe how high-quality CPR improves survival
- Explain the concepts of the Chain of Survival
- Recognize when someone needs CPR
- Perform high-quality CPR for all age groups
- Describe how to perform CPR with help from others
- Give effective breaths by using mouth-to-mouth or a mask for all age groups
- Demonstrate how to use an AED on children and adults
- Describe when and how to help someone who is choking
- Recognize the legal questions that apply to first aid rescuers

Heartsaver Terms and Concepts

In this section, you'll learn key terms and concepts that are used throughout this Heartsaver Course. They are the foundation for understanding the material presented in this workbook.

First Aid

First aid is the immediate care that you give a child with an illness or injury. This care may help an ill or injured child recover more completely or more quickly. In serious emergencies, first aid can mean the difference between life and death.

First aid may be started by anyone in any situation. Most of the time, you'll give first aid for minor illnesses or injuries. But you also may give first aid for problems that could become life-threatening. This includes applying pressure to stop moderate bleeding or giving epinephrine for a severe allergic reaction.

In this course, you will learn and practice first aid skills. This will help you remember what to do in a real emergency.

Responsive vs Unresponsive

You should know that during an emergency, it's possible that a child might become unresponsive. Here is how to decide if a child is responsive or unresponsive:

- *Responsive:* A child who is responsive will move, speak, blink, or otherwise react to you when you tap their shoulders and ask if they're OK.
- *Unresponsive:* A child who does not move, speak, blink, or otherwise react is unresponsive.

For an unresponsive child, you will learn to check whether the child needs CPR.

Agonal Gasps

A child in cardiac arrest will not be breathing or may be only gasping. When we refer to *gasps,* we mean agonal gasps. Agonal gasps are often present in the first minutes after cardiac arrest.

If a child is gasping, it usually looks like they're drawing air in very quickly. The child may open their mouth and move their jaw, head, or neck. These gasps may sound like a snort, snore, or groan. These gasps may appear forceful or weak. Some time may pass between gasps because they often happen at a slow rate.

Gasping is not regular or normal breathing. It's a sign of cardiac arrest in a child who is unresponsive.

Cardiopulmonary Resuscitation

CPR stands for cardiopulmonary resuscitation. When a child's heart stops suddenly, providing CPR can double or even triple the chance of survival. CPR is made up of 2 skills: providing compressions and giving breaths.

A *compression* is the act of pushing hard and fast on the chest. When you push on the chest, you pump blood to the brain and other organs. To give CPR, you provide sets of 30 compressions and 2 breaths.

See Part 7: CPR and AED in this workbook for more information.

Automated External Defibrillator

AED stands for automated external defibrillator. An AED is a lightweight, portable device that can detect abnormal cardiac rhythms that require treatment. It can then deliver an electrical shock to convert the rhythm back to normal.

When you give first aid, you will need to get the first aid kit and sometimes an AED. AEDs should be located in a company's main office, a building's high-traffic area, a break room, or a high-risk area like a gym—any place where most people can see and get to them in an emergency.

It's very important that you become aware of the location of the nearest first aid kit and AED. Then, you'll be able to provide the best possible first aid care to someone who is ill or injured.

Adults, Children, and Infants

This workbook presents specific Heartsaver skills and actions for helping an ill or injured child or infant until the next level of care arrives. For the purposes of this course, we use the following age definitions:

- **Adult:** Adolescent (after the onset of puberty) and older
- **Child:** 1 year of age to puberty
- **Infant:** Less than 1 year of age

Signs of puberty include chest or underarm hair on boys and any breast development for girls.

Treat anyone who has signs of puberty as an adult. If you are in doubt about whether someone is an adult or a child, provide emergency care as if the child is an adult.

Phone 9-1-1

In this course, we say, "phone 9-1-1." You may have a different emergency response number. If you do, phone your emergency response number instead of 9-1-1.

In an emergency, use the most readily available phone. This may be your cell phone or the cell phone of someone who comes to help. After phoning 9-1-1, make sure the phone is on speaker mode, if possible. This will allow the person providing emergency care to talk to the dispatcher.

Course Delivery and Options

This course will help prepare you for the most common types of first aid emergencies and equip you with CPR skills for children, infants, and adults. As part of Heartsaver Pediatric First Aid CPR AED, the American Heart Association (AHA) designed a course that is flexible in its delivery, with the most current relevant science and information. It includes core concepts that you will be required to complete. In addition to these topics, your instructor may include some optional topics. Check with your respective agency or workplace to ensure that the course or course path fulfills their requirements.

- **Heartsaver Pediatric** is designed to be flexible for students who need to review only certain topics to meet requirements for the Heartsaver Pediatric First Aid CPR AED Course. Course objectives may vary on the basis of the course topics taught.
- **Heartsaver Pediatric Total** is designed to meet licensing requirements for Occupational Safety and Health Administration (OSHA) and other regulatory agencies.

In addition to the Heartsaver Pediatric and Heartsaver Pediatric Total course options, this course may be realigned to meet the needs of many audiences. If you are a babysitter or a lifeguard, your instructor may create an agenda that will be more targeted toward your first aid and CPR AED needs. For more information on those specific path topics, refer to Table 1.

Table 1. Topic List for Course and Path Options*

Topic	Heartsaver Pediatric	Heartsaver Pediatric Total	Babysitter	Water Safety
			Recommended topics for these paths	
CPR AED				
Introduction	✓	✓	✓	✓
Child CPR AED[†]	✓	✓	✓	✓
Infant CPR[†]	✓	✓	✓	✓
Adult CPR AED[†]	Optional	Optional	Optional	Optional
Drug Overdose	Optional	Optional	Optional	Optional
Choking in Children, Infants, or Adults	✓	✓	✓	✓
First Aid Basics				
Introduction to First Aid	✓	✓	✓	✓
Assessing the Scene and Phoning for Help	✓	✓	✓	✓
Universal Precautions, Exposure to Blood, and Removing Gloves[†]	✓	✓	✓	✓
Washing Hands	✓	✓	✓	✓
Finding the Problem[†]	✓	✓	✓	✓
Medical Emergencies				
Allergic Reactions (administering an epinephrine injection[†]**)**	✓	✓	✓	✓
Asthma	✓	✓	✓	✓
Diabetes and Low Blood Sugar	Optional	✓	Optional	Optional
Seizure	Optional	✓	Optional	Optional
Heart Attack (video found in the CPR AED section, under Adult CPR AED)	✓	✓	✓	✓
Stroke (video found in the CPR AED section, under Adult CPR AED)	✓	✓	✓	✓
Fainting	Optional	✓	Optional	Optional

(continued)

Topic	Heartsaver Pediatric	Heartsaver Pediatric Total	Babysitter	Water Safety
			Recommended topics for these paths	
Injury Emergencies				
External Bleeding (controlling bleeding and bandaging†)	✓	✓	✓	✓
Shock	Optional	✓	Optional	Optional
Penetrating and Puncturing Injuries	Optional	✓	Optional	Optional
Amputation	Optional	✓	✓	✓
Bleeding From the Nose	Optional	✓	Optional	Optional
Bleeding From the Mouth	Optional	✓	Optional	Optional
Tooth Injuries	Optional	✓	Optional	Optional
Eye Injuries	Optional	✓	Optional	Optional
Internal Bleeding	✓	✓	✓	✓
Concussions	Optional	✓	Optional	Optional
Head, Neck, and Spine Injuries	Optional	✓	Optional	Optional
Broken Bones and Sprains	Optional	✓	Optional	Optional
Splinting	Optional	✓	Optional	Optional
Burns and Electrical Injuries	Optional	✓	Optional	✓
Environmental Emergencies				
Bites and Stings	Optional	✓	✓	✓
Heat-Related Emergencies	Optional	✓	✓	Optional
Cold-Related Emergencies	Optional	✓	✓	✓
Poison Emergencies	Optional	✓	✓	✓
Water Safety/ Drowning	Optional	✓	✓	✓
Prevention				
Risks of Smoking and Vaping	Optional	✓	Optional	Optional
Benefits of a Healthy Lifestyle	Optional	✓	Optional	Optional
Preventing Illness and Injury	Optional	✓	Optional	Optional

*Topic groups vary by course path. See sample agendas on the Instructor Resources website for details.
†Topic requires a skills test.

Part 1: First Aid Basics

Topics covered in this Part are

- Duties, roles, and responsibilities of the first aid rescuer
- Key steps of first aid

As you read and study this Part, pay particular attention to these 2 skills that you will be asked to demonstrate during the course:

- Removing protective gloves
- Finding the problem

Duties, Roles, and Responsibilities of the First Aid Rescuer

Your Role as a First Aid Rescuer

First aid is the immediate care that you give to a child with an illness or injury. Your role as a first aid rescuer is to

- Recognize that an emergency exists
- Make sure the scene is safe for you and the ill or injured child
- Phone or send someone to phone 9-1-1
- Provide care until someone with more advanced training arrives and takes over

Emergency Medical Services

When you phone 9-1-1, you activate the network of emergency responders—also called *emergency medical services* (EMS). Getting help on the way quickly in an emergency can save a life.

Your Duty to Maintain the First Aid Kit

The first aid kit should contain the supplies you'll need in the most common emergencies. One of the responsibilities of a first aid provider is to maintain the first aid kit and restock it after any emergency.

Determine what you should keep in your kit. See the Sample First Aid Kit in Part 5: First Aid Resources for suggestions. You may need different supplies depending on the type of facility and geographic location.

It's important that the first aid kit contain the supplies you'll need for most common emergencies. Be sure to restock it after any emergency.

How to Maintain the First Aid Kit

One responsibility of a first aid provider is to maintain the first aid kit. The kit should always contain the supplies you'll need for most common emergencies.

- Keep the supplies in a sturdy, watertight container that is clearly labeled.
- Know where the first aid kit is.
- Replace what you use so that the kit will be ready for the next emergency.
- Check the kit at the beginning of each work period for expired supplies. Make sure it's complete and ready for an emergency.

Plans for First Aid Emergencies

Every facility should be prepared for an illness or injury emergency. A plan for such emergencies includes

- The emergency response number (usually 9-1-1)
- The location of the first aid kit and AED
- The location of where medicines are stored
- Other information, such as
  - Names of people in the facility who have CPR and first aid training
  - Telephone numbers and locations of nearby emergency care facilities
  - Telephone number of the poison control center (1-800-222-1222)

First Aid Action Plans

Facilities that care for children should have a health record and written first aid action plan for each child with a medical condition. The first aid action plan describes what to do for a related medical emergency. For example, the plan gives instructions for what to do if the child has an asthma attack, a severe allergic reaction, or a seizure.

A first aid action plan usually includes

- Medical history and medicines
- Information on how and when to give the medicines
- Other actions to take if the child becomes ill
- Contact information for parents or caregivers
- Name and telephone number of the child's healthcare provider

See an example of a first aid action plan in Part 5: First Aid Resources.

Special Medical Devices

Some children with special needs may use certain medical devices. A child with diabetes, for example, may have an insulin pump. If you have a child with special needs in your care, learn about any devices the child might use and how you can help them use their device, if needed.

Plan for Storing and Managing Medicines

Make sure you know where your facility stores medicines. These medicines should be stored in a way that protects the privacy of the child and keeps them out of children's reach. Other plans may be needed for storage and management, such as checking expiration dates.

Emergency Response Plan

All schools, childcare facilities, and even families should have an emergency response plan. It's important to be prepared to respond quickly and efficiently in an emergency.

Your Responsibilities

Barriers and Benefits

Sometimes rescuers worry about doing the right thing to help in an emergency, or they may be overwhelmed by the sight of an injury.

By taking this course and learning CPR and first aid skills, you will increase your confidence and ability to respond in emergency situations so that you can help when a child or infant becomes ill or injured.

Confidentiality

As a rescuer, you will learn private things about children's medical conditions. Give information about an ill or injured child only to caregivers, healthcare providers, and anyone with more training who takes over from you.

You also may need to fill out a report if your employer or company requires it. Don't share this information, except as required. Keep private things private.

Good Samaritan Laws

If you have questions about whether it's legal to provide CPR and first aid, you should know that all states have Good Samaritan laws that protect anyone who provides first aid and CPR. The laws differ from state to state, so be sure to check the laws in your area or talk to your instructor.

Key Steps of Pediatric First Aid

The 4 key steps of pediatric first aid will guide you in caring for an ill or injured child.

The 4 Key Steps of Pediatric First Aid

For every pediatric first aid emergency, follow these 4 steps:

1. **Prevent:** Prevent children from getting hurt in the first place.
2. **Protect:** Protect yourself, and keep the ill or injured child safe from further harm.
3. **Assess**: Assess the situation, recognize the problem, and know when to phone 9-1-1.
4. **Act:** Act by giving first aid and phoning 9-1-1 if needed.

Step 1: Prevent

One of the best ways to prevent injury is to watch children and take steps to prevent an injury from happening. For example, if you see a child reach for a hot pan, you can stop them before they get burned.

Many injuries can be prevented by performing simple actions in the home, car, childcare center, school, and playground. See Part 4: Preventing Illness and Injury for more information on how to keep children safe.

Step 2: Protect

Most first aid rescuers know how important it is to protect an ill or injured child. It's also important to protect yourself. You can't help anyone if you are ill or injured yourself.

Do the following every time you give first aid care:

- Make sure the scene is safe.
- Get the first aid kit.
- Wear personal protective equipment (PPE).

Step 2 will always include these 3 actions. Do them as quickly as possible to avoid delaying care to an ill or injured child.

Make Sure the Scene Is Safe

When faced with a first aid situation, always make sure the scene is safe for you and the child before you do anything else. This is an important step. Do it every time you are providing help.

You also need to be aware of anything that might change and make it unsafe for you, the ill or injured child, and anyone else nearby. Sometimes your efforts to help can put you in danger. For example, if a child is injured in a car crash in heavy traffic, you should first make sure you can safely approach the scene.

Get the First Aid Kit

As soon as you can, you should get the first aid kit. Your first aid kit will contain PPE such as gloves and eye protection. While you are giving first aid, these help keep you safe from blood and body fluids. The first aid kit also may contain a mask for giving breaths during CPR.

Wear PPE

Wear gloves and other protective equipment as needed to protect yourself from disease and injury. Use nonlatex gloves if possible because some people are allergic to latex. Others have a sensitivity to latex that could cause serious reactions.

Step 3: Assess

Assess the Scene

As you begin to provide care, continue to assess the scene to make sure it's safe. Look around and ask yourself these questions:

- **Danger:** Is there danger for you or the ill or injured child? Move an injured child only if they're in danger or if you need to move them to safely provide first aid or CPR.
- **Help:** Are others around to help? If so, send someone to phone 9-1-1. If no one else is near, phone for help yourself.
- **Who:** Who is ill or injured? Can you tell how many people are hurt and what happened?
- **Where:** Where are you? You'll need to tell others how to get to you—in particular, the 9-1-1 dispatcher. If there are other bystanders at the scene, send one of them to meet the emergency providers and lead them to the scene.

Phone for Help

Phoning for help and getting EMS providers on the way quickly can be the most important thing to do in an emergency.

Always be aware of your location. This will help emergency providers reach you more quickly.

Make sure you know the nearest location of a phone, if a cell phone is unavailable, to use in an emergency (Figure 1). Often, the first aid kit and AED are stored at the same location as the emergency phone

Figure 1. Know the location of the nearest phone to use in an emergency. You also should know where the first aid kit and AED are stored.

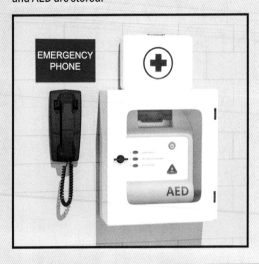

When to Phone for Help

Recognize when the child's illness or injury is serious or life-threatening. The child may need more help than you can provide. Knowing when to phone 9-1-1 is very important in providing first aid.

Your facility's emergency action plan or the child's first aid action plan may have instructions about when to phone 9-1-1. As a general rule, you should phone 9-1-1 if the child is seriously ill or injured or you are not sure what to do in an emergency.

Some examples of when you should phone 9-1-1 are if the ill or injured child

- Doesn't respond to voice or touch
- Has severe bleeding
- Has a severe allergic reaction
- Has a problem breathing
- Has a severe injury or burn
- Has received an electric shock
- Suddenly can't move a part of the body
- Has swallowed or been exposed to poison
- Has a seizure
- Has tried to commit suicide
- Has been assaulted

You will learn more about the signs and first aid actions for medical and injury emergencies later in this workbook.

How to Phone for Help

It's also important for you to know how to phone for help from your location. The easiest way to do this is with a cell phone, but you may find yourself in a situation where one is not available. In that case, do you know how to activate the emergency response number in your workplace? For example, do you need to dial 9 for an outside line? Is there an internal number to phone that will notify emergency providers who are on-site? Write the emergency response number for your location in this student workbook, in the first aid kit, and near the telephone.

For the purposes of this course, we will use 9-1-1 as the emergency response number.

Who Should Phone for Help

If other people are available, you can send someone else to phone 9-1-1 and get the first aid kit and AED. If you are alone and have a cell phone, phone 9-1-1. Put the phone on speaker mode so that you can follow the dispatcher's instructions. Here is a summary:

- If you are alone, you should
  - Shout for help
  - If no one answers and the child needs immediate care and you have a cell phone, phone 9-1-1 and put the phone on speaker mode
  - Listen to the dispatcher's instructions, such as how to give first aid, perform CPR, or use an AED

- If you are with others, you should
  - Stay with the ill or injured child and be ready to give first aid or CPR if you know how
  - Send someone else to phone 9-1-1 and get the first aid kit and AED if available
  - Have the person put the phone on speaker mode so that you can receive instructions from the dispatcher

Universal Precautions

After you assess scene safety, you should take universal precautions. These precautions are called *universal* because you should treat all blood and other body fluids as if they contain germs that can cause diseases. Other body fluids include saliva and urine.

The following universal precautions will help protect you from disease and injury:

- Wear PPE whenever necessary (Figure 2).
  - Wear protective gloves whenever you give first aid.
  - Wear eye protection if the ill or injured child is bleeding or vomiting.
  - Place all disposable equipment that has touched blood or touched body fluids containing blood in a biohazard waste bag (Figure 3) or as required by your workplace.
  - To dispose of the biohazard waste bag, follow your company's plan for disposing of hazardous waste.
  - After properly removing your gloves, wash your hands well with soap and lots of water for 20 seconds.

Figure 2. Wear protective gloves whenever you give first aid. Wear eye protection if the ill or injured child is bleeding or vomiting.

Figure 3. Place all disposable equipment that has touched body fluids, including the gloves you wore, in a biohazard waste bag if one is available. Dispose of the bag according to company policy.

Although the AHA always recommends the use of PPE and this course will often show PPE being used, it's possible that you may find yourself in an emergency where PPE is unavailable. In this situation, use your best judgement for how to render first aid.

Exposure to Blood or Other Body Fluids

You should always wear PPE whenever possible. However, if the child's blood or other body fluids do make contact with your skin, or splash into your eyes or mouth, take these steps:

- Remove your gloves if you are wearing them.
- Immediately wash your hands and rinse the contact area with soap and lots of water for 20 seconds.
- Rinse your eyes, your nose, or the inside of your mouth with plenty of water if body fluids splattered in any of these areas.
- Contact a healthcare provider as soon as possible.

Remove Protective Gloves Properly

Most of us have worn some type of glove in our lifetime, and you probably removed them without much thought. However, because of the risk of infection, using protective gloves and taking them off correctly are important safety steps. Always dispose of protective gloves properly so that anyone else who comes into contact with the biohazard waste bag will not be exposed to blood or other body fluids.

Here is the correct way to remove protective gloves (Figure 4):

- Grip one glove on the outside near the cuff and peel it down until it comes off inside out (Figure 4A).
- Cup it with your other gloved hand (Figure 4B).
- Place 2 fingers of your bare hand inside the cuff of the glove that is still on your other hand (Figure 4C).
- Peel that glove off so that it comes off inside out with the first glove inside of it (Figure 4D).
- If blood or blood-containing material is on the gloves, dispose of the gloves properly.
  - Put the gloves in a biohazard waste bag.
  - If you don't have a biohazard waste bag, put the gloves in a plastic bag that can be sealed before you dispose of it.

Always wash your hands after removing gloves in case blood or other body fluids came into contact with your hands.

Figure 4. Proper removal of protective gloves without touching the outside of the gloves.

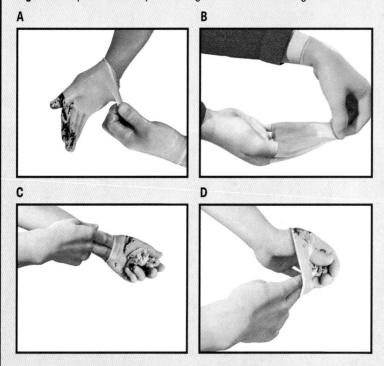

Practice Good Hand Hygiene

Even if you've been wearing protective gloves, you should always wash your hands. This is in case some blood or body fluids came in contact with your hands. Washing your hands often and not touching your face is one of the best things you can do for your health and the health of those around you, even if you haven't been exposed to blood or other body fluids.

How to Wash Hands Well

- Wet your hands with clean running water (warm if available) and apply soap.
- Rub your hands together; scrub all surfaces of hands and fingers for at least 20 seconds (Figure 5).
- Rinse your hands with lots of running water.
- Dry your hands using a paper towel or air dryer. If possible, use your paper towel to turn off the faucet.

Figure 5. Wash your hands well with soap and lots of water after taking off your gloves.

Using Waterless Hand Sanitizer

If you can't wash your hands right away, use waterless hand sanitizer. Rub your hands together so that the sanitizer covers the tops and bottoms of both hands and all fingers. Let the sanitizer air dry.

Then, as soon as you can, wash your hands with soap and water.

How Children Act When Something Is Wrong

To find out if something is wrong with a child, notice how the child is acting. Interact with the child in a calm and comforting way. Then, follow the steps for finding the problem.

Sometimes you can't tell right away if a child is ill or injured. All you may notice is that the child is not acting like themselves—that is, they're not acting the same way they usually act. This may mean that they're ill or injured.

Ill or injured children may act younger than they are. Respond to them on the basis of their behavior, not their age. To learn more about what kinds of behavior to expect from children of different ages, see How Children Act and Tips for Interacting With Them in Part 5: First Aid Resources.

Interacting With an Ill or Injured Child

Calm and comfort an ill or injured child. Here are some tips:

- **Be calm, direct, and clear:** If you are calm, you have the best chance to talk to and help a child.
  - Even infants will respond to your calm tone of voice, if not your actual words.
  - Toddlers who can usually speak well may not be able to do so in emergencies. They may bite or act angry when frustrated.
  - Adolescents may not want to talk.
  - Don't disregard a child's complaints and concerns, no matter how old the child is. Make it clear that you are listening carefully.
- **Get down to the child's level:** Kneel, squat, or sit to get down to the child's level when you talk to them. This often helps reduce the child's fear.
- **Move gently**: If a child is afraid, gentle motions may calm them.

Find the Problem

Before you give first aid, you must find out what the problem is.

- Check to see if the child is responsive or unresponsive. If the child is unresponsive, check for breathing.
- If the child is breathing and doesn't need immediate first aid, look for any obvious signs of injury, such as bleeding, broken bones, burns, or bites.
- Look for any medical information jewelry (Figure 6). This tells you if the child has a serious medical condition.
- Follow the actions outlined in Steps for Finding the Problem.

Figure 6. Look for medical information jewelry.

Steps for Finding the Problem

The following steps will help you find out what the problem is. They are listed in order of importance, with the most important step listed first.

- Make sure the scene is safe.
- Check to see if the child responds (Figure 7). Approach the child, tap their shoulders, and shout, "Are you OK? Are you OK?"
  - *If the child is responsive*
    - Ask what the problem is if the child is old enough to talk.
    - If the child only moves, moans, or groans, shout for help. Phone or send someone to phone 9-1-1 and get the first aid kit and AED.
    - Check the child's breathing.
      - If the child is breathing without difficulty and doesn't need immediate first aid, continue finding the problem.
      - If the child is having breathing problems, help them. For more information, see Breathing Problems (Asthma) in Part 2.
    - Check for any obvious signs of injury, such as bleeding, broken bones, burns, or bites.
    - Look for any medical information jewelry. This will tell you if the child has a serious medical condition.
    - Stay with the child until someone with more advanced training arrives and takes over.
  - *If the child is unresponsive*
    - Shout for help and send someone to phone 9-1-1 and get a first aid kit and AED (Figure 8).

- Stay with the child.
  - If you are alone and no one comes to help and you have a cell phone, phone 9-1-1. Put the phone on speaker mode.
- Check for breathing (Figure 9).
  - If the child is breathing, roll them onto their side (if you don't think they have a neck or back injury). Phone 9-1-1 if no one has already done so. Stay with the child until advanced help arrives.
  - If the child is not breathing or is only gasping, perform 2 minutes of CPR. Then, if no one has done so, phone 9-1-1 and get an AED (see Part 7: CPR and AED).
- Check for any obvious signs of injury, such as bleeding, broken bones, burns, or bites.
- Look for any medical information jewelry. This will tell you if the child has a serious medical condition.
- Stay with the child until someone with more advanced training arrives and takes over.

Figure 7. Tap and shout.   **Figure 8.** Shout for help.

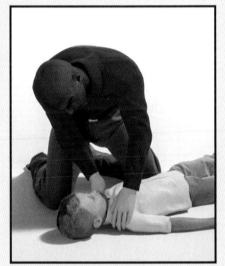
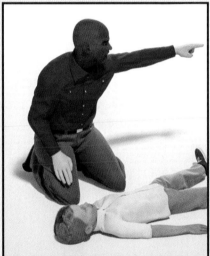

Figure 9. Check for breathing.

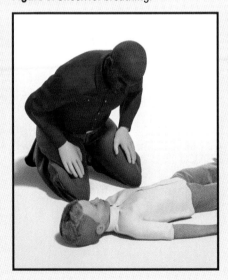

Check the Child Often

A child's condition can change quickly. A child may respond and then stop responding, so check the child often.

When a child does not respond, they may stop breathing. Watch carefully to make sure that the child keeps breathing. If the child doesn't respond and is not breathing, give CPR.

Use Caution When Moving an Ill or Injured Child

When giving first aid, you might wonder, "Should I move an ill or injured child?"

The answer is generally no. It's especially important to avoid moving a child if you suspect a head, back, spine, or pelvic injury.

However, there are times when the child should be moved, such as the following:

- If the area is unsafe for you or the ill or injured child, move to a safe location.
- If a child is unresponsive and breathing (and you don't suspect head, neck, spine, or pelvic injury), you may roll them onto their side. Rolling them onto their side may help keep the airway open in case of vomiting.

One way to move the child is to drag their clothes. Place your hands on the child's shoulders, grab their clothes, and pull them to safety.

What to Do if You Suspect Child Abuse

In many states, anyone who suspects child abuse is required to report it. By reporting what you learned, you may help protect the child from future injury and even death (see Child Abuse and Neglect in Part 5: First Aid Resources).

Step 4: Act

After you have assessed the child and found the problem, the next step is to act to provide first aid care.

We want you to act in an emergency. Sometimes, people don't act because they are afraid of doing the wrong thing. Knowing when to phone 9-1-1 is a critical part of first aid care. Two of the most important things you can do are to recognize that something is wrong and get help on the way by phoning 9-1-1.

Follow the Dispatcher's Instructions

Dispatchers—the people who answer 9-1-1 calls—can tell you what to do in serious emergencies. People with more training, such as emergency medical technicians and paramedics, usually arrive and take over not long after you call.

When you're on the phone with the dispatcher, don't hang up until the dispatcher tells you to. Answering the dispatcher's questions won't delay arrival of help.

When to Notify Parents and Caregivers

It's important to phone 9-1-1 before phoning anyone else. Notify parents and caregivers about any first aid the child received as soon as you have finished caring for the child or after advanced care arrives and takes over.

First Aid Basics: Review Questions

1. What is the most important thing that you can do in an emergency?
   a. Don't do anything unless you are sure what to do
   b. Hope someone else comes who is better prepared
   c. Phone 9-1-1
   d. Pretend you don't see the ill or injured child

2. Duties as a first aid rescuer include
   a. Maintaining the first aid kit
   b. Keeping private information about the ill or injured child private
   c. Understanding laws in your state that protect anyone who provides first aid
   d. All of the above

3. What is the most important step in preventing illness?
   a. Posting the poison control number near a phone
   b. Wearing a mask
   c. Putting all blood-containing material into a leak-proof bag
   d. Handwashing

4. The purpose of taking your gloves off properly is to keep blood or fluids on the gloves from touching your skin.
   a. True
   b. False

5. Why is it important to answer all of the dispatcher's questions?
   a. Because the 9-1-1 dispatcher needs to complete a survey
   b. Because it will get help to you as fast as possible
   c. To keep yourself safe so that you don't become injured too
   d. So the dispatcher can give a report to the media

6. When giving first aid to a child or infant, when should you phone 9-1-1?
   a. For every first aid emergency
   b. For a serious illness or injury
   c. If the child or infant has a fever and doesn't have a first aid action plan
   d. Anytime bleeding is present

7. Which of the following may be true about how a child acts when something is wrong?

  a. The child may act ill or injured

  b. The child may act younger than they are

  c. The child may need for you to talk to them on the basis of their behavior, not their age

  d. All of the above

8. If you are not sure what is wrong with a child, you'll need to find the problem. What is the first step you should take?

  a. Check for injuries or medical jewelry

  b. Check for breathing

  c. Make sure the scene is safe

  d. Check for a response (tap and shout)

Answers: 1. c, 2. d, 3. d, 4. a, 5. b, 6. b, 7. d, 8. c

Part 2: Medical Emergencies

Topics covered in this Part are

- Breathing problems (asthma)
- Allergic reactions (using an epinephrine pen)
- Dehydration
- Heart attack
- Fainting
- Diabetes and low blood sugar
- Stroke
- Seizure
- Fever

As you read and study this Part, pay particular attention to how to use an epinephrine pen, a skill that you will be asked to demonstrate during the course.

Breathing Problems (Asthma)

Asthma is a disease of the air passages that carry air into the lungs. This disease can cause mild or severe narrowing of the air passages. Asthma is common in children. When severe, it can cause life-threatening breathing problems.

Some children with asthma must take daily medicine. Others take medicine only when they have asthma symptoms. Many children with asthma have an inhaler to use when they are having breathing problems (sometimes called an *asthma attack*).

Every child with asthma should have a first aid action plan. If a child has an asthma attack, send another adult for the first aid action plan and the child's medicines.

Step 1: Prevent
- If a child in your care has asthma, be sure that there is a first aid action plan to follow in case the child develops breathing problems.
- Help the child avoid things that can trigger asthma, such as cold air, dust or pollens, and cigarette smoke.

Step 2: Protect
If possible, move the child away from the triggering environment (move away from smoke, dust, cold air)

Step 3: Assess
During an asthma attack, a child may have

- Trouble breathing
- Coughing
- Tightness in the chest
- Wheezing (whistling sound)
- Fast breathing
- Difficulty speaking more than a few words at a time (severe attack)

Step 4: Act
When a child has trouble breathing, they may panic. Younger children may not be able to use their inhalers at all, and you may need to help a child use it.

- Keep calm and soothe the child. Crying can make the asthma attack worse.
- Follow the child's first aid action plan.
- If the child has an inhaler, assemble it and help them use it.
- Phone or send someone to phone 9-1-1 if
  - The child has no medicine
  - The child doesn't get better after using their medicine
  - The child's breathing gets worse
  - The child becomes unresponsive
- Stay with the child until someone with more advanced training arrives and takes over.

Many children with medical conditions such as asthma know about their conditions and carry inhaler medicine. The medicine should make them feel better within minutes after using it.

Assemble and Use an Inhaler

Inhalers are made up of 2 parts: the medicine canister and the mouthpiece. A spacer can be attached that makes it easier for the child with the breathing problem to inhale all of the medicine (Figure 10).

Figure 10. Parts of this inhaler are the medicine canister, mouthpiece, and spacer.

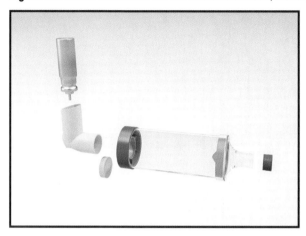

To help a child assemble and use an inhaler, follow these steps:

- Remove the cap and shake well.
- Have the child breathe out all the way.
- Have the child place the mouthpiece between their teeth and seal their lips around it.
- As they start to breathe in slowly, press down on the canister one time.
- Have them breathe in as slowly and as deeply as they can, for about 5 seconds.
- Count to 10 to allow the medicine to reach the airways of the lung.
- Repeat the steps above for each puff indicated on the inhaler, which is generally 2 puffs total.
- Replace the cap on the inhaler.

Inhalers also may come with a separate apparatus called a *spacer* or *chamber*, which is an oval plastic container that attaches to the mouthpiece of the inhaler (Figure 11). If the child's inhaler has a spacer, attach it to the mouthpiece of the inhaler after shaking but before having the child breathe out all the way.

Figure 11. Using an inhaler with a spacer.

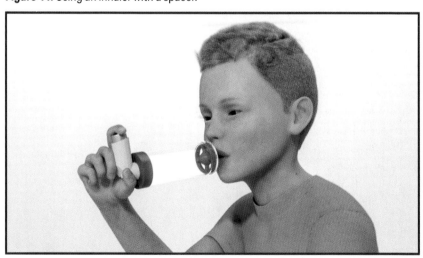

Allergic Reactions

Allergies are quite common. Allergic reaction can range from a minor irritation to a severe reaction that can quickly turn into a medical emergency.

Some things that can cause a severe allergic reaction are

- Eggs
- Peanuts
- Chocolate
- Some medicines
- Insect bites and stings, especially bee stings

Mild vs Severe Allergic Reaction

Signs of mild allergic reaction include

- A stuffy nose, sneezing, and itching around the eyes
- Itching of the skin
- Raised, red rash on the skin (hives)

Signs of severe allergic reaction include

- Trouble breathing
- Swelling of the tongue and face
- Signs of shock

Step 1: Prevent

Protect the child from things that you know the child is allergic to.

Step 2: Protect

Step 3: Assess

Figure out whether the allergic reaction is mild or severe. Watch the child carefully. Some reactions that seem mild can become severe within minutes.

Step 4: Act

If the reaction is severe, phone or send someone to phone 9-1-1. You may need to use the child's epinephrine pen as directed by the child's first aid action plan.

Epinephrine Pen for a Severe Allergic Reaction

Epinephrine is a drug that can stop a severe allergic reaction. The drug will help the child breathe more easily. In the United States, epinephrine is available by prescription in a self-injectable device called an *epinephrine pen*. People who are known to have severe allergic reactions are encouraged to carry epinephrine with them at all times.

Here are some points that you should know about epinephrine pens:

- People who carry epinephrine pens usually know when and how to use them.
- If the person needs help administering an epinephrine injection for which they have a prescription, Good Samaritan laws allow for you to help, providing you act in good faith.
- The epinephrine injection is given in the side of the thigh. It usually takes several minutes before the medicine starts to work.

- Epinephrine pens are not all alike. There are 2 doses of epinephrine pens—1 for adults and 1 for children.
- Make sure you have the epinephrine pen that belongs to that child. If the child can't use the pen themselves, and if you are allowed to, give them an injection.
- Monitor the child, and if the allergy symptoms don't get better, phone 9-1-1. You may need to administer a second dose.

Use an Epinephrine Pen

A severe allergic reaction can be life-threatening. Follow these steps to help someone with signs of a severe allergic reaction use their epinephrine pen:

- Follow the instructions on the pen. Make sure you are holding the pen in your fist without touching either end (because the needle comes out of one end). You may give the injection through clothes or on bare skin.
- Take off the safety cap (Figure 12A).
- Hold the child's leg firmly in place just before and during the injection. Press the tip of the injector hard against the side of the child's thigh, about halfway between the hip and the knee (Figure 12B).
  - Different injectors need to be held in place for different amounts of time. Be familiar with the manufacturer's instructions for the type of injector you are using. For example, EpiPen and EpiPen Jr injectors recommend holding the injector in place for 3 seconds. Some other injectors recommend holding them in place for up to 10 seconds.
- Pull the pen straight out, making sure that you don't touch the end that was pressed against the child's thigh.
- Rub or have the child rub the injection spot for about 10 seconds.
- Note the time of the injection.
- If the child doesn't get better, phone 9-1-1. If it takes more than 10 minutes for advanced help to arrive, consider giving a second dose, if available. Give the pen to the emergency providers for proper disposal.
- If possible, save a sample of what caused the reaction.

Figure 12. Using an epinephrine pen. **A,** Take off the safety cap. **B,** Press the tip of the injector hard against the side of the person's thigh, about halfway between the hip and the knee.

A

B

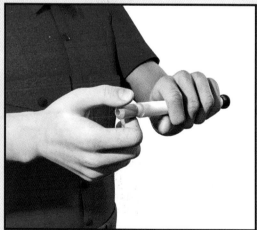

Dispose of the Epinephrine Pen Correctly

It's important to dispose of needles correctly so that no one gets stuck. Follow your company's disposal policy for sharps. If you don't know what to do, give the needle to someone with more advanced training.

Dehydration

Dehydration

A child can get dehydrated when they don't have enough fluid in their body.

How Dehydration Happens

Dehydration happens when a child loses water or fluids through

- Heat exposure
- Too much exercise
- Vomiting, diarrhea, or fever
- Decreased fluid intake

For example, a child who loses a lot of fluid through vomiting or diarrhea and doesn't drink enough to replace the fluid they have lost can become dehydrated.

Dehydration is rarely fatal in itself, but it can lead to shock, which can be fatal. It can take a little while for an ill child to lose enough fluid to go into shock.

Step 1: Prevent

- If you help a dehydrated child, you can help prevent shock.
- Make sure the child drinks and eats enough to stay hydrated.
- Seek medical treatment for conditions that can lead to excessive fluid loss like fever, vomiting, or diarrhea before the child becomes dehydrated.

Step 2: Protect

Step 3: Assess

Watch for dehydration if

- The child is vomiting, has diarrhea, or has a fever for 12 or more hours
- The child drinks less than usual

Signs of dehydration include

- Weakness
- Thirst
- Dry mouth
- Less urination than usual
- Less hunger than usual
- Dizziness

Step 4: Act

- The best first aid for dehydration is prevention: make sure the child drinks and eats enough to stay hydrated.
- If you suspect a child is dehydrated or if you see signs of shock, phone or send someone to phone 9-1-1.

Heart Attack

Heart disease is one of the leading causes of death in the world.

If someone has signs of a possible heart attack, you must act and phone 9-1-1 right away—even if the person doesn't want you to. The first minutes of a heart attack are the most important. That's when a person is likely to get worse or even die. Also, many treatments for heart attack are most successful if you give them quickly.

If a person says they have chest pain, make sure they stay calm and rest. It's best if the person doesn't drive themselves to the hospital. Stay with them until someone with more advanced training arrives and takes over.

Signs of a Heart Attack

- **Chest discomfort:** Most heart attacks involve discomfort in the center of the chest that lasts more than a few minutes or that goes away and comes back. It can feel like uncomfortable pressure, squeezing, fullness, or pain. It may be mistaken for heartburn or indigestion.
- **Discomfort in other areas of the body:** Discomfort also may appear in other areas of the upper body. Symptoms can include pain or discomfort in one or both arms or in the back, neck, jaw, shoulder, or stomach.
- **Other signs:** Other signs of a heart attack are shortness of breath (with or without chest discomfort), breaking out in a cold sweat, nausea, or light-headedness.

Signs in Women

Women may be more likely than men to experience these signs of a heart attack:

- An uncomfortable feeling in the back, jaw, neck, or shoulder
- Shortness of breath
- Nausea or vomiting

Admitting Discomfort

Many people won't admit that their discomfort may be caused by a heart attack. People often say the following:

- "I'm too healthy."
- "I don't want to bother the doctor."
- "I don't want to frighten my spouse."
- "I'll feel silly if it isn't a heart attack."

If you suspect someone is having a heart attack, act quickly and phone 9-1-1 right away. Don't hesitate, even if the person doesn't want to admit discomfort.

Actions to Take: Signs of a Heart Attack

- Make sure the person stays calm and rests. Phone or have someone else phone 9-1-1.
- Ask someone to get the first aid kit and an AED if available.
- If the person doesn't have an allergy to aspirin, serious bleeding, or signs of a stroke, have them chew and swallow 1 full-strength (adult) aspirin or 2 low-dose aspirins.
  - If you are uncertain about the person's allergies or uncomfortable giving aspirin, do not encourage the person to take aspirin.
- If the person becomes unresponsive, be prepared to give CPR and use the AED.

Heart Attack Symptoms:
Men vs Women

The most common symptom of a heart attack for both men and women is chest pain. But women may experience less obvious warning signs.

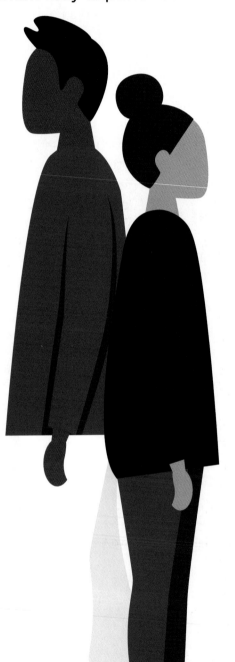

Men

Nausea or vomiting

Jaw, neck, or back pain

Squeezing chest pressure or pain

Shortness of breath

Women

 Nausea or vomiting

 Jaw, neck, or **upper** back pain

 Chest pain, **but not always**

 Pain or pressure in the **lower chest** or **upper abdomen**

 Shortness of breath

 Fainting

 Indigestion

 Extreme fatigue

Source: American Heart Association's journal, *Circulation*

Fainting

Fainting is when a child stops responding for a short period of time, usually less than a minute. After that, the child seems fine. Often, a child who faints gets dizzy and then becomes unresponsive for a short period.

How Fainting Happens

Fainting may happen when a child

- Stands without moving for a long time, especially if it's hot
- Has a heart condition
- Suddenly stands after squatting or bending down
- Receives bad news

Step 1: Prevent

If a child feels dizzy or weak, move them to a safe place and have them sit or lay down. If it's hot outside and the child is alert, it may help to give the child something cool to drink. If the child is lying down, have them cross one leg over the other and tense their leg, abdominal, and buttocks muscles. You can also have them lower their body into a squatting position and tense their abdominal muscles. Figure 13 shows certain movements someone can do that will help prevent fainting.

Step 2: Protect

Step 3: Assess

A child who is about to faint may feel dizzy, light-headed, and weak.

Step 4: Act

If a child is dizzy but still responds

- Help the child lie flat on the floor.
- Don't let the child get up too quickly.
- Put their head between their knees if they are sitting.
- Phone or send someone to phone 9-1-1 if the child doesn't improve or becomes unresponsive.
- Give CPR if the child doesn't respond and is not breathing or is only gasping.

If a child faints and then starts to respond

- Ask the child to continue to lie flat on the floor until they can sit up and feel normal.
- Make sure the child is breathing and has no injuries.
- Don't move the injured child if you suspect a head, neck, or spine injury.
- Ask the child to continue to lie flat on the floor until they can sit up and feel normal.
- If the child fell, look for injuries caused by the fall.

If the child stays unresponsive for more than 1 minute, phone 9-1-1.

Figure 13. How to help prevent fainting. **A,** Help the child lie flat on the floor. **B,** Don't let them get up too quickly. **C,** Have them put their head between their legs if they are sitting.

A

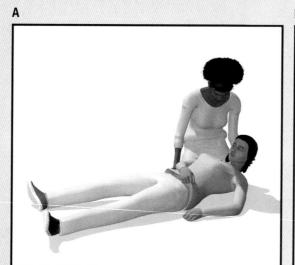

B

C

Diabetes and Low Blood Sugar

Diabetes is a disease that affects the level of sugar in the blood. Too much or too little sugar causes problems. Some children with diabetes take medicine, such as insulin, to maintain their sugar levels.

Children with diabetes who are not acting normally may have an illness or injury that is unrelated to diabetes. Be sure to check the child for other illnesses and injuries.

How Low Blood Sugar Develops

Low blood sugar can develop if a child with diabetes has

- Not eaten or has been vomiting
- Not eaten enough food for the level of activity or the insulin dose
- Injected too much insulin

Step 1: Prevent

A child with diabetes probably has specific instructions from a healthcare provider on how to manage their condition. Some of the ways a child with diabetes can prevent low blood sugar include

- Keeping track of their blood sugar
- Following a diet designed for children with diabetes
- Following the healthcare provider's directions for taking insulin

Step 2: Protect

Step 3: Assess

Signs of low blood sugar can appear quickly and may include

- A change in behavior, such as confusion or irritability
- Sleepiness or even not responding
- Hunger, thirst, or weakness
- Sweating, pale skin color
- A seizure

Step 4: Act

- Check the child's first aid action plan. Follow the plan, including directions about how to check blood sugar.
- If the child cannot sit up and swallow, phone or send someone to phone 9-1-1. Do not try to give that person anything to eat or drink.
- If the child can sit up and swallow:
  - Ask the child to swallow commercially prepared oral glucose (liquid, syrup, or gel).
  - If commercial oral glucose is unavailable, ask the person to eat or drink something with sugar that can rapidly restore blood glucose levels. These items include glucose tablets, orange juice, soft chewy candy, jelly beans, fruit leather, or whole milk.
    - For children who are awake but do not want to swallow, you can make a mixture of sugar and water and place a small amount under their tongue.
- Have the child sit quietly or lie down.
- If the child doesn't improve within 10 minutes, phone or have someone else phone 9-1-1.

Diabetic Emergency Supplies

If you are a childcare worker or teacher and a child in your care has diabetes, make sure the first aid action plan includes what to do for low blood sugar.

Children with diabetes often have emergency supplies in case of low blood sugar. Make sure the first aid action plan indicates where the supplies are located. Know how to get to them quickly in an emergency.

Stroke

Stroke is another medical emergency for which you may need to use your first aid skills. Strokes occur when blood stops flowing to a part of the brain. This can happen if a blood vessel in the brain is blocked or leaks.

For many people, getting treatment in the first hours after a stroke can reduce the damage and improve recovery. So it's important to recognize the signs of stroke quickly and get immediate medical care.

Warning Signs of Stroke

Use the F.A.S.T. method to recognize and remember the warning signs of stroke (Figure 14). *F.A.S.T.* stands for face, arms, speech, and time.

F　Face drooping: Does one side of the face droop, or is it numb?

A　Arm weakness: Is one arm weak or numb?

S　Speech difficulty: Is speech slurred?

T　Time to phone 9-1-1: If someone shows any of these symptoms, phone 9-1-1 immediately.

Figure 14. Use the F.A.S.T. method to remember the warning signs of stroke.

Actions to Take: Stroke

- Phone or have someone else phone 9-1-1 and get the first aid kit and AED.
- Note the time when the stroke signs first appeared.
- Remain with the person until someone with more advanced training arrives and takes over.
- If the person becomes unresponsive and is not breathing normally or is only gasping, give CPR.

Seizure

A seizure is abnormal electrical activity in the brain. Most seizures stop within a few minutes. Seizures often are caused by a medical condition called *epilepsy*. In infants and young children, very high fevers can cause seizures. Seizures also can be caused by a head injury, low blood sugar, and heat-related injury. Poisoning and cardiac arrest are other causes.

Signs of a Seizure

Signs of a seizure may differ. Some children who are having a seizure may

- Lose muscle control
- Fall to the ground
- Stop responding
- Have jerking movement of the arms, legs, and sometimes other parts of the body
- Lose bowel or bladder control

However, not all seizures look like this. Other children might become unresponsive. Some might just have a glassy-eyed stare.

During a seizure, children may bite their tongue, cheek, or mouth. You can give first aid for that injury after the seizure is over.

After a seizure, it isn't unusual for the child to be slow to respond and confused. The child may even fall asleep.

Step 1: Prevent

A child's first aid action plan for seizures may list possible triggers to avoid. Sometimes you can't prevent a seizure, but you can prepare for one.

Some children wet or soil their pants during a seizure. To protect a child's privacy and prevent discomfort

- Cover the child's pants with a blanket after the seizure
- Have a clean pair of pants for them to change into

Step 2: Protect

- The most important first aid action for a child having a seizure is to protect the child from injury. You may need to move toys and furniture out of the way.
- Don't put anything in the child's mouth.

Important: There are many myths about what to do when someone has a seizure. Some tell you to do things that can hurt the child who's having a seizure. (For example, putting a wooden spoon in the mouth can block breathing.) The correct information for how to help a child who is having a seizure is discussed in this workbook and during the course.

Step 3: Assess

Look for signs of seizure listed in this workbook. It's helpful for you to note the time the seizure begins and ends. Observe what happens during and after the seizure. You might need to give this information to the child's caregiver or healthcare provider.

Step 4: Act

- Move furniture or other objects out of the way.
- Remove any loose blankets around the child.
- Place a small pad or towel under the child's head.
- Phone or send someone to phone 9-1-1 if
  - This is the child's first seizure
  - You are unsure whether the child has had a seizure before
  - The first aid action plan for this child says to phone 9-1-1
  - There is more than 1 seizure in a row or seizures do not stop
  - The child is having difficulty breathing because of vomiting or fluids in the mouth
  - The child becomes unresponsive and is not breathing (also start CPR immediately)

Follow these steps to help a child after a seizure:

- Quickly check to see if the child is responsive and breathing.
- Stay with the child until someone with more advanced training arrives and takes over.
  - If the child is having trouble breathing because of vomiting or fluids in the mouth, roll them onto their side.
  - Give CPR if the child doesn't respond and is not breathing or is only gasping.

Fever

Fever is a high body temperature. It's the body's natural way of fighting illness. Fever can be caused by an illness or infection.

Some fevers are low-grade and don't need first aid. Some children with a fever may have a seizure.

Using a Thermometer

Use a thermometer that is not made of glass to take the child's temperature. Glass can break and hurt the child. You can take the child's temperature at several parts of the body. These places are recommended:

- In the armpit
- Under the tongue
- In the ear (using a thermometer made for use in the ear)
- Across the forehead

Step 1: Prevent

You can't prevent fevers, but washing hands can help prevent illnesses from spreading.

Step 2: Protect

Keep a child with a fever away from other children.

Step 3: Assess

If the child feels hot or if you suspect a child has a fever, check the child's temperature.

Step 4: Act

- Contact the parent, caregiver, or healthcare provider.
- Give medicine to reduce fever only if the child's parent, caregiver, or healthcare provider tells you to give it and approves the medicine you are giving.
- Move the sick child away from any other children to help prevent them from becoming ill.
- Phone or send someone to phone 9-1-1 if the child
  - Has a seizure
  - Has trouble breathing
  - Shows signs of shock or dehydration
  - Is hard to wake up

Aspirin Can Be Dangerous for Children

Giving aspirin to children can be very dangerous and can lead to Reye's syndrome. Only give aspirin if a healthcare provider specifically tells you to. Aspirin is different from ibuprofen or acetaminophen.

Medical Emergencies: Review Questions

1. Which of the following is true of an epinephrine pen injection?
   a. It can be given through clothes or on bare skin
   b. It should be used for every child with a rash
   c. It can only be given on bare skin
   d. It is always given in the side of the arm

2. When a child has an asthma attack, what should you do?
   a. Give the child something with sugar to drink
   b. Leave the child alone until their breathing gets better
   c. Help the child use their prescription medicine
   d. Give the child thrusts above the belly button

3. If a child with low blood sugar can sit up and swallow, give them something containing sugar to eat or drink.
   a. True
   b. False

4. What should you do if a child has a seizure?
   a. Protect the child by moving furniture or other objects out of the way
   b. Put a spoon in their mouth so they won't bite their tongue
   c. Pin them down so they will not injure themselves or scare other children
   d. Turn the child over facedown on the floor

5. What should you do if you suspect that a child has a fever?
   a. Allow the child to play with other children
   b. Check the child's temperature
   c. Put ice packs on the child
   d. Cover the child with a blanket

Answers: 1.a, 2.c, 3.a, 4.a, 5.b

Part 3: Injury and Environmental Emergencies

Topics covered in this Part are

- External bleeding
- Internal bleeding
- Burns and electrical injuries
- Heat-related emergencies
- Cold-related emergencies
- Drowning
- Amputations
- Bites and stings
- Broken bones, sprains, and bruises
- Eye injuries
- Bleeding from the nose
- Head, neck, and spine injuries
- Penetrating and puncturing injuries
- Poison emergencies
- Mouth and cheek injuries
- Tooth injuries
- Splinters

As you read and study this Part, pay particular attention to splinting, a skill that you may be asked to demonstrate during the course.

External Bleeding

Minor bleeding occurs from small cuts or scrapes. With all bleeding injuries, your first action should be to identify 2 factors to guide your care:

- The amount of bleeding
- The location of the bleeding

Minor bleeding is easily controlled, often with a simple adhesive bandage. For minor cuts anywhere on the body, wash the area with soap and water, and then apply a dressing to the wound. Once the bleeding has stopped, you can apply an antibiotic ointment, if the person has no known allergies, and an adhesive bandage. This method has been proven to help wounds heal faster and more effectively.

If the wound is bleeding more than can be easily stopped with an adhesive bandage, you will need to determine whether it is non–life-threatening or life-threatening bleeding.

Consider a wound to be life-threatening if the flow of blood is continuous and steady and if the volume of loss appears large, equal to about half of a 12-ounce can. You don't want to wait for blood to accumulate to take action because cuts that may seem more moderate at first can become severe if the person is on certain types of blood-thinning medications, like aspirin. It's important to not underestimate the amount of blood loss; be prepared to take action.

Phone or ask someone else to phone 9-1-1 if

- There is a lot of bleeding
- You cannot stop the bleeding
- You see signs of shock
- You suspect a head, neck, or spine injury
- You are not sure what to do

Direct Pressure and Bandaging

Many people confuse the terms *dressing* and *bandage*. Here is what they mean and how they work together:

- A *dressing* is a clean material used directly on a wound to stop bleeding. It can be a piece of gauze or any other clean piece of cloth.
- A *bandage* is material used to protect or cover an injured body part. A bandage can also be used to help keep pressure on a wound.

If necessary, you can hold gauze dressings in place over a wound with a bandage (Figure 15).

Figure 15. Using dressings and a bandage on a wound. **A,** Apply dressings over the bleeding area, and put direct pressure on the dressings. Use the heel of your hand to apply pressure directly to the wound. **B,** Place a bandage over the dressings.

A

B

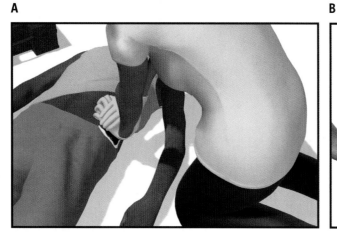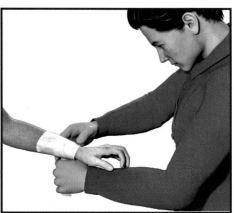

When to Phone 9-1-1 for Bleeding

Phone or send someone to phone 9-1-1 if

- There is a lot of bleeding
- You cannot stop the bleeding
- You see signs of shock (see Shock later in this Part)
- You suspect a head, neck, or spine injury
- You are not sure what to do

Step 1: Prevent

- Use the Child and Infant Safety Checklist (Table 2) to help keep a child safe.
- Use dressings to help prevent infection.
- Use antibiotic cream on small scrapes and surface cuts to prevent infection. (Make sure the child doesn't have an allergy to antibiotic cream first.)

Step 2: Protect

If the injured child can help you, ask them to put direct pressure on the wound while you put on your PPE.

Step 3: Assess

Find the place that's bleeding.

Step 4: Act

Apply dressings over the bleeding area and put direct pressure on the dressings.

- Use the heel of your hand to apply pressure directly to the wound.
- If the bleeding is not life-threatening, apply a dressing to the bleeding area.
  - Put direct pressure on the dressings using the heel of one hand, with the other hand stacked on top of the first. If possible, keep your arms straight while applying pressure downward onto the wound. Direct pressure should be firm, steady, and constant.
- Do not remove pressure from the wound to add more dressings. Also, do not remove a dressing once it's in place because this could cause the wound to bleed more. Continue holding firm pressure until help arrives or the bleeding stops. Releasing pressure too soon can allow the wound to start bleeding again.
- If the bleeding does not stop, press harder. Keep pressure on the wound until it stops bleeding.
- Once the bleeding stops, or if you cannot keep pressure on the wound, wrap a bandage firmly over the dressings to hold them in place.
- A child who is bleeding should be seen by a healthcare provider as soon as possible because the child may need stitches or a tetanus shot.

Use a Tourniquet

If an arm or leg has severe bleeding and you can't stop the bleeding with direct pressure, you can use a tourniquet. Be sure you phone 9-1-1 and get an AED, if available. Uncontrolled bleeding can lead to more complications.

The first aid kit may contain a commercial tourniquet. If applied correctly, a tourniquet should stop the bleeding. Tightening the tourniquet may cause pain but will minimize blood loss. If you need to apply a tourniquet, the injury is serious enough that you should phone 9-1-1.

Once you have the tourniquet in place, note the time. Leave it alone until someone with more advanced training arrives and takes over.

How to Apply a Manufactured Tourniquet

Follow these steps to apply a premade tourniquet from your first aid kit (Figure 16):

- Make sure the scene is safe.
- Phone or send someone to phone 9-1-1 and get the first aid kit (if you don't already have it) and an AED.
- Wear PPE.
- Apply the tourniquet 2 to 3 inches above the bleeding site.
- Do not place the tourniquet on a joint.
- Pull the free end of the tourniquet to make it as tight as possible, and then secure it.
- Twist the windlass, or knob, until bleeding stops.
- You need to twist the windlass as tight as possible to stop the life-threatening bleeding. This may cause the child discomfort or pain.
- Secure the windlass in the clip and note the time the tourniquet was applied.
- Once you have the tourniquet in place and the bleeding has stopped, leave it alone until someone with more advanced training arrives and takes over.
- If a manufactured tourniquet is not available, and direct manual pressure with or without the use of a hemostatic dressing (a wound dressing containing an agent that promotes blood clotting) does not stop life-threatening bleeding, a first aid provider trained in the use of an improvised tourniquet may consider using one.

- If the bleeding is severe and is located on a body part that is not the arm or leg, such as the head, neck, chest, abdomen, shoulders, or hips, you can pack the wound and then apply pressure as noted above. *Packing the wound* means to take a material like gauze or clothing and place it tightly into the wound (Figure 17). You would then apply pressure and a compression dressing.

Figure 16. Using a manufactured tourniquet. **A,** Put direct pressure on the dressings using the heel of one hand, with the other hand stacked on top of the first. Direct pressure should be firm, steady, and constant. **B,** Apply the tourniquet 2 to 3 inches above the bleeding site on the person's arm or leg, closer to the heart. **C,** Pull the free end of the tourniquet to make it as tight as possible, and then secure it. **D,** Twist the windlass, or knob, as tight as possible until the bleeding stops. **E,** Secure the windlass and note the time the tourniquet was applied.

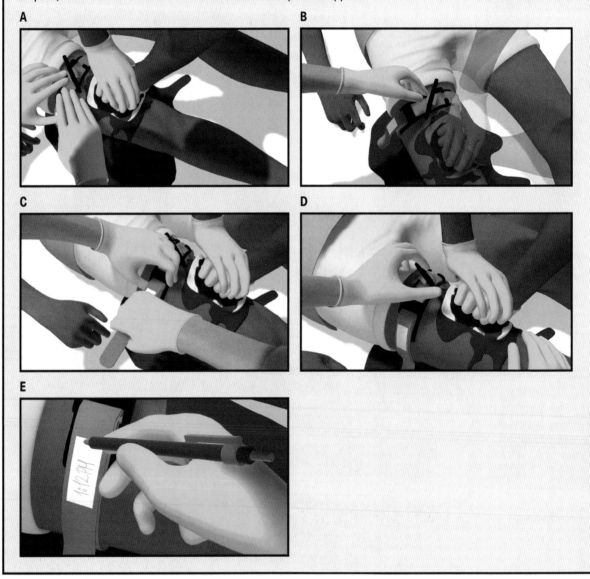

Figure 17. Packing the wound. **A,** Pack the wound with gauze or a clean cloth. **B,** Place it tightly in the wound. **C,** Continue to apply direct pressure until the bleeding stops.

A

B

C

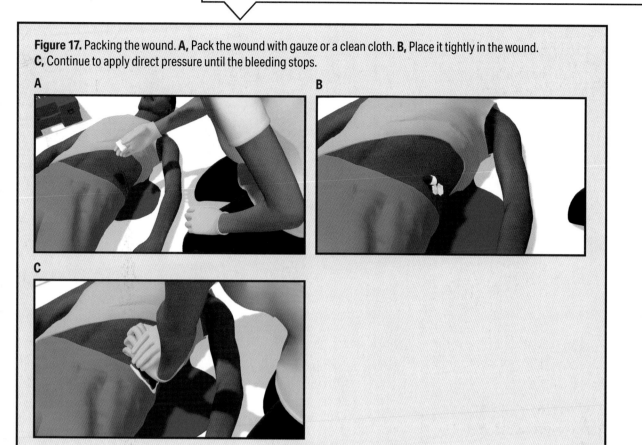

Shock

Shock can happen when someone loses a large amount of blood or water and when not enough blood flows to the most important parts of the body. It's not an illness a child can just "get." Another illness or injury always causes it. Shock can happen quickly in children and can be fatal.

Watch for shock if a child

- Has recently lost a lot of fluid, such as with vomiting or diarrhea
- Has a fever and has not taken in enough fluid
- Loses a lot of blood, including bleeding inside the body
- Has a severe allergic reaction

Step 1: Prevent

Use the Child and Infant Safety Checklist (Table 2) to help prevent injuries that lead to severe bleeding or fluid loss.

Step 2: Protect

Get the AED along with the first aid kit.

Step 3: Assess

Children in shock don't act like themselves. Signs of shock include

- Feeling weak, faint, or dizzy
- Being nauseated
- Breathing very fast
- Acting restless, confused, or unusually sleepy
- Looking pale
- Being cold to the touch

Step 4: Act

- Phone or send someone to phone 9-1-1 and get the first aid kit and AED.
- Help the child lie down on their back.
- Cover the child with a blanket to keep them warm (Figure 18).
- Stay with the child until someone with advanced training arrives and takes over.
- Give CPR if the child doesn't respond and is not breathing.

Figure 18. Cover a child who is in shock.

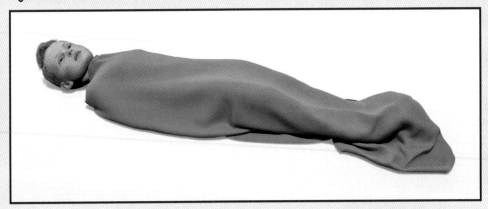

Internal Bleeding

Internal bleeding is bleeding inside the body. The skin may not be broken, so you may not be able to see blood or signs of bleeding. But something (an organ, a blood vessel) beneath the skin is cut, bruised, or torn and is bleeding inside the body. This kind of blood loss is serious. It can lead to shock.

When to Suspect Internal Bleeding

You should suspect internal bleeding if a child has

- An injury from a car crash (you may see seatbelt marks)
- Been hit by a car
- Fallen from a height
- An impact to the abdomen or chest (struck by a blunt object; you may see bruising)
- Sports injuries, such as slamming into other players or being hit with a ball
- Pain in the abdomen or chest after an injury
- Shortness of breath after an injury
- Coughed up or vomited blood after an injury
- Signs of shock without external bleeding
- A knife or a gunshot wound

Step 1: Prevent

Use the Child and Infant Safety Checklist (Table 2) to help prevent injuries that may lead to internal bleeding.

Step 2: Protect

Phone or send someone to phone 9-1-1 and get an AED.

Step 3: Assess

A child with internal bleeding may develop shock (see signs of shock in the Shock section).

Step 4: Act

- Have the child lie down and keep still.
- Check for signs of shock.
- Phone or send someone to phone 9-1-1.
- Give CPR if the child doesn't respond and is not breathing.

Burns and Electrical Injuries

Burns

Burn injuries can be caused by contact with heat, electricity, or chemicals. Heat burns are caused when anyone comes in contact with a hot surface, hot liquids, steam, or fire.

The only thing you should put on a burn is cool water and clean dressings—never use ice. Ice can damage a burned area.

If the child has a burn, keep the child warm. If a skin burn is large, a child may not be able to control body temperature effectively. If the child gets too cold, low body temperature (hypothermia) can develop. A healthcare professional should evaluate anyone who has burns that involve

- Large areas of the body
- The face, neck, hands, or genitalia
- Blistering or broken skin
- Difficulty breathing

Step 1: Prevent

Take steps to prevent heat burns, chemical burns, and sunburns.

Preventing Heat Burns

- Keep hot foods and drinks out of children's reach.
- Don't hold a child or infant when cooking or working with something very hot.
- Make sure food isn't too hot before feeding it to children, especially infants.
- Be careful with small heating appliances or tools that have hot surfaces, such as curling irons.
  - Keep the appliance out of children's reach.
  - Keep the cords out of reach so that children can't pull the appliance down.
  - Unplug appliances and tools when not in use.
- Adjust the hot water heater so that the water is 120° Fahrenheit or cooler. This will prevent scalding a child in a short time.
- Check the water temperature before allowing a child to get into it.

Preventing Chemical Burns

Keep chemicals, such as bleach and drain cleaner, out of children's reach.

Preventing Sunburn

- Keep infants younger than 6 months out of direct sunlight.
- Try to keep children out of the sun between 10 AM and 4 PM.
- For children older than 6 months, use sunscreen made for children.
- Put sunscreen on children 30 minutes before they go outside.
- Choose a water-resistant or waterproof sunscreen with a sun protection factor (SPF) of at least 15. The product should block both ultraviolet A and ultraviolet B rays.
- Reapply waterproof sunscreen every 2 hours. This is especially important if children are playing in the water.
- Have children wear sun-protective clothing such as a hat or SPF shirt to further protect from the sun.

Step 2: Protect

Move the child out of the sun or away from a potentially dangerous scene.

Step 3: Assess

If the child or their clothing is on fire, immediately attempt to put it out:

- Have the child stop, drop, and roll.
- Then, cover the child with a wet blanket until the fire is out.
- Assess the burned area to see if the burn is large or small.

Step 4: Act

For small burns

- Cool the burned area immediately with cold (but not ice-cold) water for at least 10 minutes.
- If you don't have cold water, use a cool or cold (but not freezing) clean compress.
- Run cold water on the burn until it doesn't hurt (Figure 19).
- You may loosely cover the burn with a dry, nonstick sterile or clean dressing.

For large burns

- If there is a fire, the burn area is large, or you're not sure what to do, phone or send someone to phone 9-1-1.
- If the child or their clothing is on fire, put the fire out. Have the child stop, drop, and roll. Then, cover the child with a wet blanket.
- Once the fire is out, remove the wet blanket. Carefully remove jewelry and clothing that is not stuck to the skin.
- Cool the burn area immediately with cold (but not ice-cold) water for at least 10 minutes.
- After you cool the burns, loosely cover them with dry, nonstick sterile or clean dressings.
- Cover the child with a dry blanket.
- Check for signs of shock.
- See a healthcare provider for burns that involve
  - Large areas of the body
  - The face, neck, hands, or genitalia
  - Blistering or broken skin
  - Difficulty breathing

Figure 19. Run cold water on a burn until it doesn't hurt.

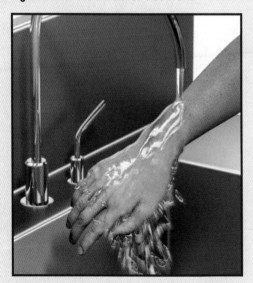

Many people have heard about different ointments for burns. The only thing you should put on a burn is cool water and clean dressings unless you are given other instructions by a healthcare provider.

Electrical Injuries

Electricity can cause burns on the outside of the body and on the inside, injuring organs. You may see marks or wounds where the electricity has entered and left the body. The damage can be severe. But there's no way to tell how severe on the basis of the marks on the outside of the body. Electricity can stop a child from breathing. It can cause a deadly abnormal heart rhythm and cardiac arrest.

If an electrical injury is caused by high voltage, like a fallen power line, phone 9-1-1. Don't enter the area or try to move wires until the power has been turned off.

Step 1: Prevent

- Install shock stops (plastic outlet plugs) or outlet covers on all electrical outlets.
- Make sure cords are not frayed or cracked.
- Make sure plugs fit properly into the outlets.

Step 2: Protect

- Get an AED along with the first aid kit.
- Use caution before touching the child.
  - Don't touch the child if they're still in contact with the power source. Electricity can travel from the power source through the child to you. It's best to turn the power off, but only attempt this if you are trained to do so. Once the power is off, you may touch the injured child.
  - Don't touch anything that is in contact with a fallen power line or other high-voltage source. Electricity can travel through anything that comes in contact with a high-voltage source (even a wooden stick). Wait until the power has been turned off to enter the area. Then, provide help.
  - Don't touch the child if they are lying in water and still in contact with the power source. Electricity can travel through water.

Step 3: Assess

Look for burns and other injuries. Electricity may leave only small marks on the body or multiple visible injury sites. You can't tell how much damage there is inside the body by looking at the marks on the outside of the body.

Step 4: Act

Use caution before touching the child (see Step 2: Protect).

- Phone or send someone to phone 9-1-1.
- When it's safe to touch the injured child, give CPR if the child doesn't respond and is not breathing or is only gasping. Use an AED if available.
- A healthcare provider should check anyone who has an electrical injury as soon as possible.

Heat-Related Emergencies

Most heat-related emergencies are caused by vigorous exercise in a warm or hot environment. Children and infants have more trouble than adults do in keeping their bodies at the right temperature.

Heat-related emergencies include

- Heat cramps
- Heat exhaustion
- Heat stroke

If the child does not get first aid care for heat cramps or heat exhaustion, their condition can get worse and progress to heat stroke, which is a life-threatening emergency.

Heat Cramps

Heat cramps are painful muscle spasms. They usually occur in the calves, arms, stomach muscles, and back.

Step 1: Prevent

- Heat cramps are caused by dehydration. Make sure the child drinks water or sports drinks before and while playing outside in hot weather. Avoid sugary drinks because these lead to further dehydration.
- Avoid playing outside when temperatures are very hot.
- See Heat Exhaustion for more steps in preventing heat-related illness.

Step 2: Protect

Move the child out of the heat to a cooler location.

Step 3: Assess

Assess the child for

- Muscle cramps
- Sweating
- Headache

Heat cramps are a sign that the child needs first aid care. Heat-related problems can get worse and be life-threatening.

Step 4: Act

- Have the child rest and cool off.
- Have the child drink water or sports drinks with electrolytes.
- If the child can tolerate it, apply a bag with ice and water wrapped in a towel to the cramping area until the child cools down.

Heat Exhaustion

Although heat exhaustion is not life-threatening, it can quickly become heat stroke. Heat stroke is life-threatening. Heat exhaustion is caused by dehydration. It often happens when a child exercises in the heat and sweats a lot.

Step 1: Prevent

Children should stay hydrated before and after exercise.

- During exercise, children should drink water or sports drinks often to stay hydrated.
- Children should wear lightweight, light-colored clothes when exercising in the sun or heat.
- Children should take frequent breaks while exercising or playing in heat.
- If it's very hot or humid, children should avoid exercising outdoors.
- Children should exercise during cooler times of the day.
- Carefully watch children who are not fit or are not used to exercising in the heat.
- If a child looks ill or not normal (not like themselves), have them stop exercising.
- Check for signs of heat exhaustion or heat stroke.

Step 2: Protect

Move the child to a cooler area.

Step 3: Assess

Look for the following signs of heat exhaustion:

- Sweating
- Nausea
- Dizziness
- Vomiting
- Muscle cramps
- Feeling faint or fatigued

Step 4: Act

- Have the child lie down in a cool place.
- Remove as much of the child's clothing as possible.
- Cool the child with a cool (but not ice-cold) water spray. If cool water spray isn't available, place cool damp cloths on the neck, armpit, and groin area.
- If the child is responsive and can drink, have the child drink water or something with sugar and electrolytes, such as juice or a sports drink.

Heat Stroke

Heat-related conditions can progress quickly if not recognized and treated. Heat stroke is a dangerous condition that is life-threatening.

It's important to begin cooling a child who might have heat stroke immediately—every minute counts. If you can't put the child into cool (but not ice-cold) water up to their neck, try to cool them with a cool water spray or cool wet towels.

If the child starts behaving normally again, stop cooling them. If you cool the child too much, it can lead to low body temperature.

Step 1: Prevent
- Follow the same prevention steps as for heat exhaustion.
- Giving first aid to a child who has heat exhaustion will help keep heat exhaustion from becoming heat stroke.
- Never leave a child or infant in a hot car. See the Child and Infant Safety Checklist (Table 2) for tips on car safety.

Step 2: Protect
- Get an AED along with the first aid kit.
- Move to a cooler area.

Step 3: Assess
Look for the following signs of heat stroke:
- Confusion or unresponsiveness
- Passing out
- Dizziness
- Seizure
- Feeling faint or fatigued
- Nausea, vomiting
- Muscle cramps

Step 4: Act
- Phone or send someone to phone 9-1-1.
- Put the child in cool (but not ice-cold) water up to their neck if possible. If not available, spray them with cool water, apply cool wet towels, or use ice packs to cool the child.
- Give CPR if the child doesn't respond and is not breathing or is only gasping.

Cold-Related Emergencies

Cold-related emergencies may involve the whole body or only part of the body. Cold injuries include low body temperature and frostbite.

Low Body Temperature

Cold injury to the whole body is called *low body temperature* or *hypothermia.* Hypothermia happens when body temperature falls. This is a serious condition that can cause death.

Here are some key points to remember about hypothermia:

- A child can develop hypothermia even when the temperature is above freezing. For example, a child can get hypothermia from walking in the rain and wind without a jacket.
- Very small children and infants can easily develop hypothermia.
- Shivering protects the body by producing heat. Shivering stops when the body becomes very cold.

Step 1: Prevent
- Make sure children wear appropriate clothing in cold weather.
- Watch small children closely if they are in very cold weather to make sure they stay warm and dry.

Step 2: Protect
- Get an AED along with the first aid kit.
- Move to a warmer area.

Step 3: Assess
Look for signs of hypothermia, which include
- Skin that's cool to the touch
- Shivering, which stops when the body temperature is very low
- Confusion or drowsiness
- Personality changes
- Sleepiness and lack of concern about this condition
- Stiff, rigid muscles and skin that becomes ice-cold and blue
- Slowed breathing

As the child's body temperature continues to drop, it may be hard to tell if they're breathing. The child may become unresponsive and even appear to be dead.

Step 4: Act
- Get the child out of the cold.
- Phone or send someone to phone 9-1-1 if you suspect hypothermia.
- Remove wet clothing, pat the child dry, and cover with a blanket.
- Put dry clothes on the child.
- Cover the child's body and head, but not the face, with blankets, towels, or even newspapers.
- Stay with the child until someone with more advanced training arrives and takes over.
- Give CPR if the child doesn't respond and is not breathing or is only gasping.

Frostbite

Frostbite affects parts of the body that are exposed to the cold, such as fingers, toes, nose, and ears.

Frostbite typically happens outside in cold weather. But it can also happen inside when children without gloves handle ice or other extremely cold materials.

Step 1: Prevent

- Make sure children wear appropriate clothing in cold weather.
- Watch small children closely if they are in very cold weather to make sure they stay warm.

Step 2: Protect

Move to a warmer area.

Step 3: Assess

The signs of frostbite include the following:

- The skin over the frostbitten area is white, waxy, or grayish-yellow.
- The frostbitten area is cold and numb.
- The frostbitten area is hard, and the skin doesn't move when you push on it.

Step 4: Act

- Move the child to a warm place.
- Phone or send someone to phone 9-1-1 and get the first aid kit.
- Remove tight clothing and jewelry from the frostbitten part.
- Remove wet clothing and pat the child's body dry.
- Put dry clothes on the child and cover them with a blanket.

Caution

- Do not try to thaw the frozen part if you think there may be a chance that it will freeze again before the child can get to medical care.
- Do not rub the frostbitten area because it can cause damage. If you need to touch the area, do so gently.

Water Safety/Drowning

Drowning is a leading cause of preventable death in children younger than 15 years. Children are very attracted to water; they can drown if they enter the water without adult supervision.

Shallow Water

Young children and infants can drown in very shallow water, such as a 5-gallon bucket or the bathtub. This is because their heads are very heavy compared with the rest of their body. If a small child or infant leans over and falls into a bucket, toilet, or small container, they may not be able to lift their head out of the water.

Step 1: Prevent

Do not leave a child alone around any water.

- Swimming pools, creeks, fountains, lakes, and rivers are very appealing to most children. It's important to closely watch all children near pools or other bodies of water.
- Any child or infant can drown, even if they know how to swim.
- Always stay within reach of a child when near a body of water.
- Use life jackets when appropriate.
- See the Child and Infant Safety Checklist (Table 2) for more ways to prevent drowning.

Step 2: Protect

Get an AED along with the first aid kit.

Step 3: Assess

If a child is wet and not breathing, the child may have drowned.

Step 4: Act

- If the child is under water, safely remove the child from the water.
- Send someone to phone 9-1-1.
- Give CPR if the child doesn't respond and is not breathing or is only gasping.
- After 5 sets of compressions and breaths, phone 9-1-1 and get an AED (if no one has done this yet).
- If the child doesn't need CPR, remove wet clothing and wrap the child in dry blankets.
- Continue to check if the child needs CPR.
- Children who drown in cold water may not be breathing and may have cold, blue skin and stiff muscles. Even if the child appears dead, start CPR right away. Continue until someone with more advanced training arrives and takes over.

Amputation

One injury that may seem overwhelming is traumatic amputation.

Amputation happens when any part of the body is cut or torn off. It may be possible to reattach certain body parts, so it's important to know what to do. First, stop bleeding by applying pressure. You may need to use a tourniquet if bleeding is severe. Then, protect the amputated part.

Treating Amputation

You can preserve a detached body part at room temperature, but it will be in better condition to be reattached if you keep it cool.

Step 1: Prevent

Use the Child and Infant Safety Checklist (Table 2) to prevent injuries that may lead to amputation.

Step 2: Protect

Step 3: Assess

- Assess the injury.
- Find the part of the body that has been amputated.

Step 4: Act

- Phone or send someone to phone 9-1-1.
- Stop the bleeding from the injured area with pressure. You may have to press for a long time with very firm pressure to stop the bleeding.
- Stay with the injured child until someone with more advanced training arrives and takes over.

If you find the amputated part, follow these steps:

- Rinse the amputated part with clean water (Figure 20A).
- Cover it with a clean dressing.
- Place it in a watertight plastic bag (Figure 20B).
- Place the bag in another container with ice or ice and water (Figure 20C).
- Label it with the injured child's name, the date, and the time.
- Make sure the body part gets to the hospital with the injured child.

Remember: Do not place the amputated body part directly on ice because extreme cold can injure it. Always put something in between a body part and the ice and water.

Figure 20. A, If you can find the amputated part, rinse it with clean water. **B,** If it will fit, place the wrapped part in a watertight plastic bag. **C,** Place that bag in another labeled bag that contains ice or ice and water.

A

B

C

Bites and Stings

Bites and stings are common injuries to children. The risk of many animal and insect bites and stings will vary according to location and time of year. For example, scorpions are found in dry climates. Ticks are a problem in wooded areas. Marine animals live in or near the ocean.

Be familiar with the bites and stings that happen most often in your area. Sometimes, children are bit or stung by venomous animals. *Venomous* means that the animal can inject a toxic substance (or poison) into the skin when they bite or sting. Be prepared to give first aid care.

Human and Animal Bites

Young, preschool-aged children sometimes bite each other. Some young children will bite others to show their feelings. Most children stop biting when they grow older.

Animal bites are less common and often can be prevented. Unfortunately, when they do happen, animal bites can be serious.

When a bite breaks the skin, the wound can bleed. It may become infected from the germs in the child's or animal's mouth. Bites that don't break the skin usually are not serious.

Not only is the bite a concern, but there can be a risk of rabies from dogs or wild animals. Rabies in wild animals is most often reported in raccoons, skunks, and bats. Dogs bitten by infected animals can also become infected.

Step 1: Prevent
- Take precautions to protect children from bites (see the Child and Infant Safety Checklist [Table 2]).
- Some bites get infected. You can help prevent this by washing small wounds well as soon as possible.

Step 2: Protect

Stay away from any animal that acts strangely.

Step 3: Assess

Find where the child was bitten.

Step 4: Act
- Wash the wound with plenty of soap and water.
- Stop any bleeding with pressure or bandages.
- If there is a bruise or swelling, place a bag of ice and water wrapped in a towel on the bite for up to 20 minutes.
- For all bites that break the skin, contact a healthcare provider as soon as possible.

Risk of Rabies

Animals that may carry rabies include cats, dogs, skunks, raccoons, foxes, bats, or other wild animals. Always contact a healthcare provider right away for any bite that breaks the skin.

Also, because of the increased risk of contracting rabies from bats, anyone who has had direct contact with a bat should contact a healthcare provider as soon as possible.

Snakebites

Bites from venomous snakes are a first aid emergency. If a child has been bitten by a snake, try to identify the type of snake. This can help with treatment. Sometimes you can tell what type of snake it is from the color or bite mark. But if you're not sure, assume that the snake is venomous.

Step 1: Prevent
- Teach children to stay away from snakes and leave them alone. Teach them to tell an adult when they see a snake.
- Keep outdoor play areas away from places where snakes can live. This includes tall grass or piles of rock or firewood.
- Teach children not to reach into places where snakes may hide.

Step 2: Protect
- Be very careful around any snake, even if it's wounded. Back away and go around the snake.
- If a snake has been hurt or killed, do not handle it. A snake can bite even when badly hurt or close to death.
- If a snake needs to be moved, use a long-handled shovel. If you don't need to move it, leave it alone.

Step 3: Assess
Look for these signs that a child has been bit by a venomous snake:
- Pain at the bite area that keeps getting worse
- Swelling of the bite area
- Nausea, vomiting, sweating, or weakness

Step 4: Act
- Ask another adult to move any other people away from the area. Phone or send someone to phone 9-1-1.
- Ask the injured child to stay still and calm and to avoid moving the part of the body that was bitten.
- Remove any tight clothing and jewelry.
- Gently wash the area with running water and soap.
- Keep the child still and calm until someone with more advanced training arrives and takes over.
- If one is available, apply a dressing with a bandage over the bite to provide pressure. Make sure the bandage is wrapped snugly around the area with the bite but loose enough that you can slide a finger under the dressing.

You may have heard other ways to give first aid for a snakebite, such as sucking out the poison (venom). Don't do that. Follow the steps listed in this workbook to give first aid care for a snakebite.

Bee Stings and Insect and Spider Bites

Usually, insect bites and stings cause only mild pain, itching, and swelling at the bite. However, some insect bites can be serious and even fatal if
- Venom is injected into the child from the bite or sting
- The child has a severe allergic reaction to the bite or sting

Bees are the only insects that leave behind their stingers. If a child gets stung by a bee, look for the stinger and remove it.

Step 1: Prevent

Take the following steps to prevent insect bites and stings:

- Keep children from bothering insects.
- Use insect repellent that is approved for use on children.
- If you know a child has a severe allergy to an insect or bee sting, keep their epinephrine pen close by at all times. This is especially important when the child is outdoors.
- Have children wear light-colored clothing when they are in areas where insects are likely to be. Their clothing should cover their arms and legs.
- Keep flowering plants and gardens away from areas where children play.
- Put outdoor toys away so that spiders and insects can't hide inside them.

Step 2: Protect

Step 3: Assess

Find the area that has been bitten or stung. Try to figure out if the bite is poisonous.

The bite or sting of insects that aren't venomous can cause mild signs of redness and itching at the bite area. However, the bite of a venomous spider or scorpion can cause a child to become ill.

Signs that a child has been bit by a venomous spider or scorpion are

- Severe pain at the site of the bite or sting
- Muscle cramps
- Headache
- Fever
- Vomiting
- Breathing problems
- Seizures
- Unresponsiveness

Step 4: Act

Follow these steps to help a child who was bitten or stung by a nonvenomous insect, bee, or spider:

- If the child was stung by a bee, scrape the stinger and venom sac away with something hard and dull that won't squeeze it—like the edge of a credit card or photo ID card. (Squeezing the venom sac can release more poison.)
- Wash the sting or bite area with running water and soap.
- Watch the child for at least 30 minutes for signs of a severe allergic reaction. Be prepared to use the child's epinephrine pen if needed.
- Put a bag of ice and water wrapped in a towel over the area for up to 20 minutes.

Children who have had severe allergic reactions to an insect bite or sting usually have an epinephrine pen and know how to use it. They often wear medical identification jewelry.

Follow these steps to help a child with a known allergy to bees who was bitten or stung (even if you're not sure the child was stung by a bee):

- Get the first aid kit and the child's epinephrine pen.
- If the child develops a severe allergic reaction, phone or send someone to phone 9-1-1.
- Use the skills you learned earlier to help the child inject epinephrine by using their epinephrine pen. Be prepared to help the child. Give a second injection of epinephrine if needed.

Follow these steps to help a child who was bitten or stung by a venomous spider or scorpion or who shows signs of a bite or sting that might be from a venomous spider or scorpion:

- Phone or send someone to phone 9-1-1.
- Wash the bite with lots of running water and soap.
- Put a bag of ice and water wrapped in a towel on the bite or sting.
- Keep the child still and calm until someone with more advanced training arrives and takes over.

Tick Bites

Ticks are found on animals and in wooded areas. They attach themselves to exposed body parts. Many ticks are harmless, but some carry serious diseases.

If you find a tick, remove it as soon as possible. The longer the tick stays attached to a child, the greater the child's chance of catching a disease.

Step 1: Prevent

- Wear proper clothing.
  - Children should wear light-colored clothing so that you can see the tick more easily later.
  - Clothing should cover a child's arms and legs. Tuck pants into the child's socks or boots.
- Take precautions in wooded or brushy areas.
  - Children should avoid wooded areas with dead leaves and other debris. They also should avoid brushy areas with high grass. These areas are home to many insects, especially ticks.
  - Children should stay on the trails when walking through wooded or brushy areas.
- Use insect repellent safely.
  - Insect repellent products containing DEET may be used on children over 2 months old if the label says it's safe for use on children.
  - Select a repellent that contains no more than 30% DEET.
  - Use DEET products only on infants older than 2 months.
  - Do not use sunscreen containing DEET because DEET should be applied only once a day while sunscreen should be reapplied frequently throughout the day. Do not use products containing lemon eucalyptus oil on children younger than 3 years.
- Be careful when using insect repellent.
  - Don't spray the repellent on the child. Instead, apply to your own hands. Then, rub it on the child.
  - Avoid putting repellent on children's hands, around the eyes, or on cut or irritated skin.
  - Do not allow children to handle insect repellents.
  - After returning indoors, wash the child's treated skin or bathe the child.
  - Wash clothes exposed to insect repellents with soap and water.

Step 2: Protect

Check the child's hair and skin after being in areas where ticks are found.

Step 3: Assess

Find the tick bite.

Step 4: Act

- Use tweezers to grab the tick by its mouth or head, as close to the skin as possible.
- Try to avoid pinching the tick.

- Lift the tick straight out. If you lift the tick until the child's skin tents and wait for several seconds, the tick may let go.
- Place the tick in a plastic bag so that the caregiver can take it to the healthcare provider if needed.
- Wash the bite with running water and soap.
- See a healthcare provider if the child is in a region of the country where tick-borne diseases occur.

You may have heard about other ways to remove a tick. The correct way to remove a tick is to follow the steps in this workbook.

Marine Bites and Stings

You've learned that it's important to be aware of ticks and other insects and animals when you're in the wilderness. It's just as important to be aware of marine fish and animals when at the beach or swimming in the ocean.

Bites and stings from jellyfish, stingrays, or stonefish can cause pain, swelling, redness, or bleeding. Some marine bites and stings can be serious. They can even be fatal if a child has a severe allergic reaction to the sting or the venom.

Step 1: Prevent
- At the beach, watch for signs that warn you about dangerous jellyfish or other marine life.
- Even dead marine animals can sting. Avoid touching them with bare hands or skin.

Step 2: Protect
Try to avoid touching a biting or stinging marine animal. But if you must, use something to protect your bare skin.

Step 3: Assess
The following are signs of a bite or sting from a venomous or poisonous marine animal:

- Chest pain
- Cramps
- Fever
- Weakness, faintness, or dizziness
- Nausea or vomiting
- Numbness or trouble moving parts of the body
- Severe pain and swelling
- Color changes of the skin in the area bitten or stung

Step 4: Act
- Keep the injured child quiet and still.
- Wipe off stingers or tentacles with a gloved hand or towel.
- If the sting is from a jellyfish, rinse the injured area for at least 30 seconds with lots of vinegar. If vinegar isn't available, use a baking soda and water solution instead.
- Put the part of the body that was stung in hot water. You also may have the child take a shower with water as hot as they can bear for 20 minutes or as long as pain persists.
- Phone or send someone to phone 9-1-1 if
  - A child has been bitten or stung by a marine animal and has signs of a severe allergic reaction
  - A child was bitten or stung in an area known to have venomous marine animals
- For all bites and stings that break the skin, contact a healthcare provider as soon as possible.

Broken Bones, Sprains, and Bruises

Broken bones, sprains, and bruises are common first aid emergencies. Joint sprains happen when joints move in directions they're not supposed to. A child may get a bruise if they get hit or run into a hard object. Bruises happen when blood collects under the skin. They can appear as red or black-and-blue spots.

Treating Broken Bones, Sprains, and Bruises

It's hard to tell whether a bone is broken or a joint is sprained without an x-ray. You'll give the same first aid care for both injuries.

Step 1: Prevent

Use the Child and Infant Safety Checklist (Table 2) to help prevent injuries that may lead to broken bones, sprains, and bruises.

Step 2: Protect

Remove jewelry from the injured area if possible.

Step 3: Assess

Assess the injured area for broken bones or sprains. Signs include

- Swelling
- Pain
- Not being able to move the injured part
- A joint turning slightly blue

Step 4: Act

- Cover any open wound with a clean dressing.
- Put a towel on top of the injured body part. Place a bag filled with ice and water on top of the towel over the injured area (Figure 21). Keep the ice in place for up to 20 minutes. If ice isn't available, you can use a bag of frozen vegetables or a cold pack. But it will not be as cold and may not work as well as ice and water.
- If the injured body part hurts, the child should avoid using it until checked by a healthcare provider.
- Phone or send someone to phone 9-1-1 if
  - There is a large open wound
  - The injured body part is abnormally bent
  - You're not sure what to do

Figure 21. Put a plastic bag filled with ice and water on the injured area with a towel between the ice bag and the skin.

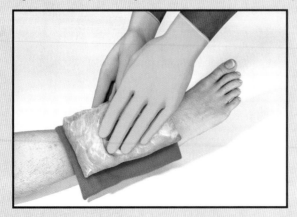

Splinting

A splint keeps an injured body part from moving (Figure 22). If a broken bone has come through the skin or is bent, it shouldn't be straightened. The injury needs to be protected until someone with more advanced training arrives and takes over.

Figure 22. A splint keeps an injured body part from moving.

If the injured part is bleeding, apply direct pressure to stop the bleeding. Put a dressing on the wound before applying the splint.

Leave bent and deformed body parts in their bent or deformed positions as you apply the splint. If a broken bone has come through the skin, cover the wound with a clean dressing. Splint as needed.

Phone or send someone to phone 9-1-1 if

- There is a large open wound
- The injured part is abnormally bent
- You're not sure what to do

Step 1: Prevent

Use the Child and Infant Safety Checklist (Table 2) to help prevent injuries that may lead to broken bones.

Step 2: Protect

Step 3: Assess

Most of the time, splints are applied by a healthcare provider. However, sometimes you may need to splint an arm or a leg. For example, if you are hiking in the wilderness and a child breaks an arm, you may need to apply a splint. A splint will help keep the injury from getting worse until the child can get medical care.

Step 4: Act

- Find an object that you can use to keep the injured arm or leg from moving.
  - Rolled-up towels, magazines, and pieces of wood can be used as splints. Splint in a way to reduce pain and limit further injury. The splint should be longer than the injured area. It should support the joints above and below the injury.
- After covering any broken skin with a clean or sterile cloth, tie or tape the splint to the injured limb so that it supports the injured area (Figure 23).
- Use tape, gauze, or cloth to secure it. It should fit snugly but not cut off circulation.
- If you're using a hard splint, like wood, make sure you pad it with something soft, like clothing or a towel.
- Keep the limb still until the injured child can be seen by a healthcare provider.

Figure 23. Use stiff material, such as a rolled-up magazine, to splint injured body parts.

If you don't have anything to use as a splint for an injured arm, the child can use their other arm to hold the injured one in place. To help an injured child self-splint an arm, have them place their hand across their chest and hold it in place with their other arm.

Eye Injuries

Eye injuries in children can happen at home, at school, or during play.

How Eye Injuries Happen

Some common eye injuries in children happen from a

- Direct hit or punch to the eye or to the side of the head
- Direct hit from a ball or other object
- High-speed object (such as a BB gun pellet)
- Stick or other sharp object that punctures the eye
- Small object, such as a piece of dirt, that gets in the eye

Step 1: Prevent

Some ways that you can prevent eye injury are the following:

- Be sure that children wear proper eye protection when playing sports.
- Monitor toys with eye safety in mind.
- Keep objects that can cause eye injury, such as rubber bands or pointed scissors, away from children. Supervise them very closely when they do use these objects.
- Keep chemicals and sprays out of reach.

Step 2: Protect

Step 3: Assess

Assess the eye for signs of injury, such as

- Pain
- Trouble seeing
- Bruising
- Bleeding
- Redness, swelling

Step 4: Act

- If something small like sand gets in a child's eye, rinse with lots of running water.
- Phone or send someone to phone 9-1-1 if the
  - Object doesn't come out
  - Child complains about extreme pain
  - Child still has trouble seeing
- Tell the child to keep their eyes closed until someone with more advanced training arrives and takes over.

Bleeding From the Nose

Nosebleeds are common in children.

How Nosebleeds Happen

Some reasons for nosebleeds are injury, irritation, and picking the nose.

Step 1: Prevent
Use the Child and Infant Safety Checklist (Table 2) to help prevent injuries that lead to bleeding from the nose.

Step 2: Protect

Step 3: Assess
Assess the child to find the source of the bleeding.

Step 4: Act
- Have the child sit and lean forward.
- Pinch the soft part of the nose on both sides (Figure 24) with a clean dressing.
- Place constant pressure on the nostrils for a few minutes until the bleeding stops. If bleeding continues, press harder.
- Phone or send someone to phone 9-1-1 if
  - You can't stop the bleeding in about 15 minutes
  - The bleeding is heavy, such as gushing blood
  - The injured child has trouble breathing

Figure 24. Press on both sides of the nostrils. Have the child lean forward.

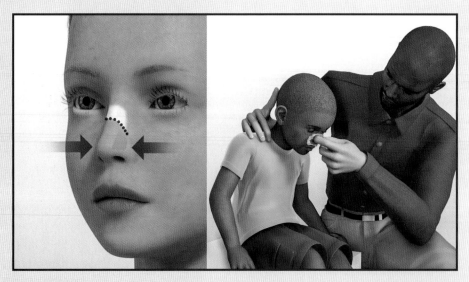

First Aid Myth

A child with a nosebleed should lean forward, not backward. Leaning backward will not help stop the bleeding. You will see less blood when a child tilts their head back, but this is because the blood drains down the child's throat. Swallowed blood can lead to vomiting.

Head, Neck, and Spine Injuries

With any kind of head, neck, or spine injury, be cautious about moving an injured child.

Suspect a head, neck, or spine injury if the child

- Fell from a height
- Was injured by a strong blow to the head
- Was injured while diving
- Was involved in a car crash
- Was riding a bicycle or motorbike involved in a crash, especially if the helmet broke in the crash or the child was not wearing a helmet

Signs of a Head Injury

If you think a child has a serious head injury, phone or send someone to phone 9-1-1. Suspect a head injury if an injured child

- Does not respond or only moans
- Acts sleepy or confused
- Vomits
- Has trouble seeing, walking, or moving any part of the body
- Has a seizure

A child should be evaluated by a healthcare or EMS provider as soon as possible if their signs and symptoms get worse, if there's a change in responsiveness, or if you have other causes for concern.

If the child becomes unresponsive, be sure that someone has phoned 9-1-1. Give CPR if the child is not responding and not breathing or is only gasping.

A child with signs of a head injury should not play sports, ride a bike, or do similar activities until a healthcare provider says it's OK.

Concussion

A concussion is a type of head injury. Concussions usually happen because of falls, motor vehicle crashes, and sports injuries. A concussion may happen when the head or body is hit so hard that the brain moves inside the skull.

Possible signs of concussion are

- Feeling stunned or dazed
- Confusion
- Headache
- Nausea or vomiting
- Dizziness, unsteadiness, or difficulty in balance
- Double vision or flashing lights
- Loss of memory of events that happened before or after the injury

If a child has a head injury and any of these signs, contact a healthcare provider right away. Phone or send someone to phone 9-1-1 if a child with a head injury

- Loses consciousness
- Has a change in level of consciousness—for example, becomes sleepier or more irritable
- Has a progression of signs—for example, is alert at first and then becomes confused, speaks clearly at first and then begins to mumble, or is sleepy and gets sleepier instead of waking up
- Has other causes for concern

Spine Injury

If a child falls, an injury to the spine is possible. The bones of the spine protect the spinal cord, and the spinal cord carries messages between the brain and the body.

If the spine is damaged, the spinal cord may be injured. The child may not be able to move their legs or arms. They may lose feeling in parts of the body.

Suspect possible spine damage if the child

- Was in a car or bicycle crash
- Fell from a height
- Has tingling or is weak in the hands and feet
- Has pain or tenderness in the neck or back
- Appears "drunk" or not fully alert
- Has other painful injuries, especially of the head or neck

Step 1: Prevent

Falls are a leading cause of head, neck, and spine injuries. Use the Child and Infant Safety Checklist (Table 2) to help keep a child safe from falls.

Step 2: Protect

- Get an AED along with the first aid kit.
- Try not to move the child. If you must move the child, use caution. Do not twist or turn the head or neck unless it's necessary to do any of the following:
  - Turn the child faceup to give CPR
  - Move the child out of danger
  - Reposition the child because of breathing problems, vomiting, or fluids in the mouth

Step 3: Assess

Check an injured child for the signs of head injury, concussion, and spine injury listed earlier in this section.

Step 4: Act

- Phone or send someone to phone 9-1-1 and get the first aid kit and the AED.
- Have the child remain as still as possible.
- Do not twist or turn the child's head or neck unless absolutely necessary (see Step 2: Protect earlier in this section).
- Stay with the person until advanced help arrives.

With a head, neck, or spine injury, you may have to control external bleeding. This is why it's important to get the first aid kit. Getting the AED is also important. If the child's condition gets worse, you may need to give CPR until someone with more advanced training arrives and takes over.

Penetrating and Puncturing Injuries

First aid for penetrating and puncturing injuries is different from more common bleeding injuries.

How Penetrating and Puncturing Injuries Happen

An object such as a knife, nail, or sharp stick can wound a child by penetrating the body or puncturing the skin. If the object is stuck in the body, leave it there until a healthcare provider can treat the injury. Taking it out may cause more bleeding and damage.

Step 1: Prevent

- Supervise children closely whenever they are near common household items that can cause puncture injuries.
- Don't let children play with sharp sticks or toys with sharp points.
- Use the Child and Infant Safety Checklist (Table 2) to help prevent penetrating and puncturing injuries.

Step 2: Protect

- Get an AED along with the first aid kit.
- Don't try to pull the object out.

Step 3: Assess

Find the place on the child's body where the object has gone in.

Step 4: Act

- Phone or send someone to phone 9-1-1.
- Take steps to stop any bleeding you can see. Do not try to remove the object if it is stuck in the body.
- Try to keep the injured child from moving until advanced care arrives and takes over.

Poison Emergencies

A poison is anything that can cause sickness or death if a child swallows it, breathes it, or gets it in the eyes or on the skin. Many medicines, household products, and even some plants can poison children.

Poison Control Hotline

The phone number for the poison control center should be in the first aid kit or clearly posted in the areas where chemicals are used.

Contact your local poison center by phoning the American Association of Poison Control Centers (Poison Control) at 1-800-222-1222.

Questions the Poison Control Center Dispatcher May Ask

When you phone the poison control center, they may ask for the following information:

- What is the name of the poison?
- Can you describe it if you can't name it?
- How much poison did the child touch, breathe, or swallow?
- How old is the child?
- How much does the child weigh?
- When did the poisoning happen?
- How is the child feeling or acting now?

Step 1: Prevent

To prevent poisonings, keep items that might be dangerous out of children's reach. Some examples include

- All medicine, including vitamins and supplements
- Mouthwash
- Essential oils
- Cleaning supplies
- Chemicals

Use the Child and Infant Safety Checklist (Table 2) to help prevent poisoning.

Step 2: Protect

- Get an AED along with the first aid kit.
- Take actions to make sure the scene is safe in a poison emergency.
  - Look for signs that warn you that poisons are nearby (Figure 25).
  - Look for spilled or leaking containers.
  - If there is a chemical spill or the child is in an unsafe area, try to move the child to an area with fresh air (if you can do so safely).
  - If the scene seems unsafe, do not approach. Tell everyone to move away.
  - Stay out of the scene if you see multiple people who may have been poisoned.

Figure 25. Look for symbols of poisons, such as these.

Some places have a safety data sheet, or SDS, that describes how a specific chemical or poison can be harmful. It may have first aid recommendations as well.

Step 3: Assess

Suspect that a child has been poisoned if

- You see empty containers that used to hold dangerous contents, such as pill, vitamin, or perfume bottles
- A child's breath or body has a chemical smell
- You suspect the child has eaten parts of a plant
- You smell something in the room with the child that might be poisonous or dangerous

Step 4: Act

For a child who has swallowed poison:

- Move the child away from the poisonous substance. Take the box, bottle, can, or leaf with you for reference when talking to the 9-1-1 dispatcher.
- Phone or send someone to phone 9-1-1.
- Answer the dispatcher's questions (see Questions the Poison Control Center Dispatcher May Ask earlier in this Part).
- Tell the dispatcher the name of the poison if you know it. Some dispatchers may connect you to a poison control center.
- Give only those antidotes that the poison control center or dispatcher tells you to. The first aid instructions on the poison itself can be helpful but may be incomplete.
- Give CPR if the child doesn't respond and is not breathing or is only gasping. Use a mask for giving breaths. This is especially important if the poison is on the child's lips or mouth.
- Follow these steps to help a child who has poison on the skin or in the eyes:

For a child who has poison on the skin or in the eyes:

- Move the child from the scene of the poison to an area with fresh air if you can.
- As quickly and as safely as possible, wash or remove the poison from the child's skin and clothing. Help the child to a faucet, a safety shower, or an eyewash station.
- Remove clothing and jewelry from any part of the body touched by the poison. Use a gloved hand to brush off any dry powder or solid substance from the child's skin (Figure 26A).
- Run lots of water over the affected area until someone with more advanced training arrives and takes over.

- If an eye is affected, ask the child to blink as much as possible while rinsing the eyes. If only one eye is affected, make sure the eye with the poison in it is lower than the other eye when you rinse (Figure 26B). This will keep the poison from getting into the unaffected eye.
- Give CPR if the child doesn't respond and is not breathing or is only gasping. Use a mask for giving breaths. This is especially important if the poison is on the child's lips or mouth.

Figure 26. Remove poisons. **A,** Brush off any dry powder or solid substances. **B,** Rinse the eye.

A

B

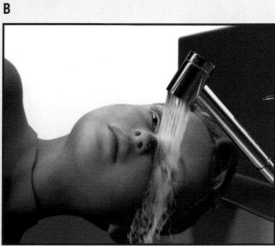

Mouth and Cheek Injuries

A mouth injury can be serious if blood or broken teeth block the airway and cause breathing problems.

Treating Mouth and Cheek Injuries

Bleeding from the mouth can usually be stopped with pressure.

Step 1: Prevent

Not all mouth and cheek injuries can be prevented, but you can create a safe environment through proper supervision. Use the Child and Infant Safety Checklist (Table 2) to help prevent injuries.

Step 2: Protect

Watch for trouble breathing. Sometimes bleeding in the mouth can block the airway.

Step 3: Assess

Locate the source of the bleeding. The injured area may be inside or outside of the mouth.

Step 4: Act

If bleeding is coming from the tongue, lip, or cheek and you can reach it easily, apply pressure with gauze or a clean cloth (Figure 27).

- Phone or send someone to phone 9-1-1 if
  - You can't stop the bleeding in 5 to 10 minutes
  - The child is having trouble breathing

Figure 27. If the bleeding is from the tongue, lip, or cheek, press the bleeding area with sterile gauze or a clean cloth.

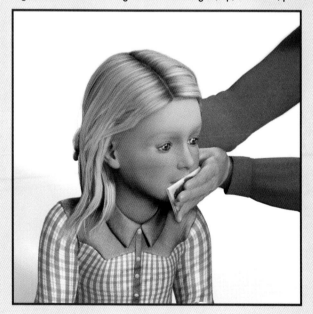

Tooth Injuries

Children with a mouth injury may have broken, loose, or knocked-out teeth. These teeth can be a choking hazard, especially for young children.

Treating Tooth Injuries

When a child injures a permanent tooth, sometimes the tooth can be saved. To save the tooth, the child needs immediate first aid care and emergency dental care.

Step 1: Prevent

- Take action to prevent falls.
- Make sure children wear appropriate protective equipment such as mouth guards when playing sports.
- Use the Child and Infant Safety Checklist (Table 2) to help prevent tooth injuries.

Step 2: Protect

If the child has knocked out a tooth, give first aid care and then find the tooth. Hold the tooth by the crown, not the root. Care for the tooth as described in Step 4.

Step 3: Assess

- Check the child's mouth for any missing teeth, loose teeth, or parts of teeth.
- If the child has lost a baby tooth, a small amount of bleeding is normal.

Step 4: Act

- Check the child's mouth for any missing or loose teeth or parts of teeth.
- If a tooth is chipped, gently clean the injured area. Contact a dentist.
- If a tooth is loose, have the child bite down on a piece of gauze to keep the tooth in place. Contact a dentist.
- If a tooth has come out, it may be possible for a dentist to reattach the tooth. When you hold the tooth, hold it by the crown—the top part of the tooth (Figure 28). Don't hold it by the root because you may injure it.
- Apply pressure with gauze to stop any bleeding in the empty tooth socket.
- Clean the area where the tooth was located with saline or clean water.
- Put the tooth in an oral rehydration salt solution or, if not available, store it in cling wrap. If these aren't available, store the tooth in the injured child's saliva.
  - To do this, have the child spit into a container. Then, put the tooth in the container. Do not have the child hold the tooth in their mouth.
- Immediately take the injured child and tooth to a dentist or emergency department.
- Phone or send someone to phone 9-1-1 if you can't control the bleeding.

If a baby tooth is knocked out, stop any bleeding with pressure. Then, contact a dentist. You don't need to put the tooth in a solution to preserve it.

Figure 28. Hold the tooth by the crown.

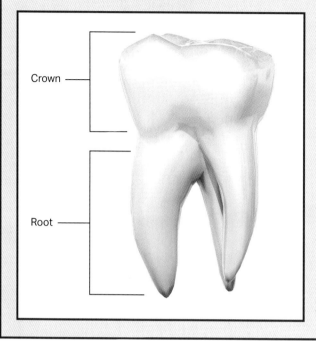

Crown

Root

Splinters

Splinters are small pieces of wood or metal that stick under the skin. Usually, you won't need to phone 9-1-1 for a splinter.

Step 1: Prevent
Supervise children if there is a risk that they may get a splinter, such as on wooden playground equipment.

Step 2: Protect

Step 3: Assess
Find the splinter.

Step 4: Act
- Try to remove the splinter. Keep it dry. If the splinter gets wet, it will be harder to remove in one piece.
  - If the splinter is small, put sticky tape over the splinter. Then, pull the tape off.
  - If tape doesn't pull it out, hold the end of the splinter with clean tweezers. Gently pull it out without digging.
- After you remove the splinter, clean the child's wound with water and soap if available.
- If you can't get a splinter out, leave it in. Clean the area with soap and water. Get medical care if the splinter
  - Is large
  - Is deeply embedded in the skin
  - Is difficult to remove
  - Is in the eye
  - Broke off, possibly leaving part of it in the wound
  - Becomes infected

Injury and Environmental Emergencies: Review Questions

1. What can stop most severe bleeding?
   a. Putting on gloves
   b. Putting direct pressure on the wound
   c. Applying an antibiotic cream
   d. Having the child lie down

2. Which of the following should be used as a dressing?
   a. A clean cloth
   b. A cold pack
   c. A dirty cloth
   d. A piece of tape

3. Shock happens when a child has lost too much blood or water.
   a. True
   b. False

4. What should you do if a child has an injury that needs to be splinted?
   a. Place a plastic bag filled with warm water on the area to reduce swelling
   b. Apply a splint only after an x-ray confirms that the bone is broken
   c. Ideally, place the splint so that it supports the joints above and below the injury
   d. Straighten the injured body part before using a splint

5. What should you do when a child gets a small burn?
   a. Cool the area with cold, but not ice-cold, water
   b. Cover the area with lots of cold cream and butter
   c. Put the child in a bathtub filled with ice
   d. Run warm water on the burn until it doesn't hurt

6. Which of the following is true of electrical injuries?
   a. Electrical injuries have no effect on the heart
   b. Electrical injuries never cause injury inside the body
   c. High-voltage electricity can travel through everything that touches the power line or source
   d. All electrical injuries should be treated with ice

7. Which of the following is true of heat stroke?

   a. Heat stroke can quickly turn into heat exhaustion

   b. Heat stroke is not dangerous

   c. Heat stroke can be caused by exercising outside when the weather is very warm or hot

   d. Heat stroke should be treated with warm water

8. How can a child get hypothermia (low body temperature)?

   a. From walking in rain and wind without a jacket

   b. On a hot, sunny day

   c. When they don't have enough sugar in their blood

   d. After a seizure

9. In which of the following can a young child drown?

   a. A 5-gallon bucket

   b. A toilet

   c. A bathtub

   d. All of the above

10. What is the most important thing to do for a child with a suspected head, neck, or spine injury?

    a. Have the child sit up

    b. Help the child walk around

    c. Do not twist or turn the head or neck

    d. Give the child a sports drink

11. If a child has a penetrating injury, you should remove it as quickly as possible.

    a. True

    b. False

12. What should you do if a child has a permanent tooth knocked out?

    a. Always hold the tooth by the crown

    b. Put the tooth in an oral rehydration salt solution or cling wrap

    c. Immediately take the child and tooth to a dentist or emergency department

    d. All of the above

13. What should a child with a nosebleed do?

    a. Lie flat on the ground, facedown

    b. Lean backward as you apply pressure on the soft part of the nose

    c. Blow their nose and then hold an icepack on the back of their neck

    d. Lean forward as you apply pressure on the soft part of the nose

Answers: 1.b, 2.a, 3.a, 4.c, 5.a, 6.b, 7.c, 8.a, 9.d, 10.c, 11.b, 12.d, 13.d

According to the Centers for Disease Control and Prevention, injuries are the leading cause of death in children. Common childhood injuries include car accidents, falls, and drowning.

You can help prevent illness and injury to children. Look for possible dangers. Take simple actions to keep children safe. Go to **cdc.gov/safechild** for more information.

Topics covered in this Part are

- Car safety and prevention
- Indoor safety and prevention
- Outdoor safety and prevention

For more ways to improve safety and prevent injury, see the Child and Infant Safety Checklist (Table 2).

Car Safety and Prevention

Injuries from motor vehicle crashes are a leading cause of death in children in the United States. Many of these deaths can be prevented by use of properly installed car seats, booster seats, or seat belts.

Car Seats

Car seats help prevent injuries during car crashes.

Here are some guidelines for using car seats:

- Make sure it fits the child. Select a car seat based on the child's age, height, and weight.
- Get it installed correctly. It should not move more than 1 inch side to side or back to front. Local child car seat inspection stations are available to inspect the car seat. Technicians will make sure it's installed correctly. They will teach you how to install it. In most cases, this service is free. Go to **www.safercar.gov** for more information and to find a location near you.
- Use it correctly. Straps should fit snugly and securely.
- Use it regularly. Children should be in a car seat each time they ride in a car. Keep the child in the car seat as long as recommended. Know the height and weight requirements for child safety seat use in your state.

See the Child and Infant Safety Checklist (Table 2) for more information on car seats, booster seats, and seat belts.

Safety in and Around Cars

To help prevent injuries and be safe in the car, remember the following:

- Everyone should wear seat belts.
- All children younger than 13 years should ride in the back seat.
- Never leave a child alone in the car.
- Teach children how to cross streets safely.
- Children should hold hands with or be carried by an adult in parking lots or other places where cars are moving and drivers might not see a child walking.
- Children should cross streets at crosswalks. Teach them street-crossing safety.

For a more complete checklist of things you can do to improve car safety, see the Child and Infant Safety Checklist (Table 2).

Indoor Safety and Prevention

There are many things that you can do to help keep children safe indoors. Below are some actions to take to prevent poisoning and reduce the risk of sudden infant death syndrome (SIDS). See the Child and Infant Safety Checklist (Table 2) for other important actions to take to prevent falls, burns, and other injuries.

Prevent Poisoning

Some basic actions to prevent injury from poisoning are to

- Keep children away from things that can hurt them, such as medicine, cleaning products, essential oils, and other poisonous liquids.
- Install smoke and carbon monoxide detectors, and keep working batteries in them.
- Post the poison control center number (1-800-222-1222) near a phone. Add this number to your contacts list in your cell phone.

In a poisoning emergency, phone or send someone to phone 9-1-1. The dispatcher can send help right away if needed and connect you to the poison control center.

Reduce the Risk of SIDS

SIDS is the sudden death of an infant younger than 1 year that is not explained by other causes.

In the United States, SIDS is a leading cause of death among infants 1 to 12 months old. Although deaths from SIDS have decreased since 1990, rates for some ethnic groups are still high.

To help reduce the risk of SIDS, do the following:

- Put infants to sleep on their back.
- Make sure the bed has only a mattress, a fitted sheet, and the infant.
    - This means no bumper pads, extra blankets, or stuffed toys.
- Put infants to sleep in their own bed. Infants should not sleep in their parents' bed or with another child, including a sibling, because they could suffocate.

Other Actions for Indoor Safety

Here are some other actions for improving indoor safety:

- Install window guards to keep windows from opening completely.
- Put baby gates at the top and bottom of stairs.
- Supervise children to prevent falls.
- Watch children near water. Infants and young children can drown in bathtubs and toilets.
- Never shake or play roughly with an infant. Shaking or tossing an infant in the air while playing can cause serious injury.

Outdoor Safety and Prevention

There are many things that you can do to help keep children safe outdoors. Here are some actions to take for sports safety and water safety. See the Child and Infant Safety Checklist (Table 2) for other important actions to take to keep children safe, including when using bikes and skateboards.

Sports Safety

Many childhood injuries happen on the playground. Others happen while children are playing organized sports. Do the following to help keep children safe during play:

- Remove any broken glass or trash from playground areas.
- Have children wear closed-toe shoes.
- Protect children from sunburn.
- In very hot or cold weather, protect children from heat- or cold-related injuries.
- Before a child starts to play a new organized sport, the parents or caregivers should check with a healthcare provider. It's important to identify any health issues that might put the child at risk for illness or injury.
- Children should wear appropriate safety equipment, such as mouth guards and helmets.

Water Safety

Infants and young children can drown in lakes and pools. Drowning can happen in only a few inches of water. Do the following to help reduce the risk of drowning:

- Never leave a child alone around any water.
- An adult must always supervise children while they swim. Never allow a child to swim alone.
- Ensure that home swimming pools have fences. Fencing should be at least 4 feet high on all sides. They should have self-closing, self-latching gates. This includes a gate between the home and the pool.
- Children should wear life jackets in boats and at other times as needed.

Other Actions for Outdoor Safety

Here are some other actions for improving outdoor safety:

- Teach children how to handle and care for a pet.
- Teach children how to behave around dogs, such as
  - Avoiding unfamiliar dogs
  - Asking the owner first before approaching or petting
- Use insect repellent that is approved for use on children.
- Keep children from bothering insects.
- If a child has a known insect allergy, keep their epinephrine pen available whenever they play outside.

Child and Infant Safety Checklist

Millions of children are seen for injuries each year in US emergency departments. Injuries are the leading cause of death among children.

Safety checklists can help you identify risks for injury at home, in the car, at childcare facilities, at schools, and on playgrounds. Safety checklists also tell you what to do to reduce risk. But these only reduce risk. There is no such thing as a risk-free environment. That's why it's important to learn first aid.

Review Table 2 to determine which precautions you already take and which ones require you to take action.

Table 2. Child and Infant Safety Checklist

Action	I follow this safety precaution	Purchase of safety item is required
Car safety: car seats and seat belts		
Birth to 12 months A child younger than 1 year should always ride in a rear-facing car seat. There are different types of rear-facing car seats: • Infant-only seats can only be used rear facing. • Convertible and 3-in-1 car seats typically have higher height and weight limits for the rear-facing position. These allow you to use a rear-facing seat for a longer period of time.		
1 to 4 years Keep a child in a rear-facing car seat as long as recommended. Know the height and weight requirements for child safety seat use in your state. Once the child outgrows the rear-facing car seat, the child is ready to travel in a forward-facing car seat with a harness. The car seat should be placed in the back seat of the automobile.		
4 to 6 years Keep a child in a forward-facing car seat with a harness until they reach the maximum height or weight limit. Once the child outgrows the forward- facing car seat with a harness, it's time to travel in a booster seat. The booster seat should still be in the back seat.		
6 to 12 years Keep a child in a booster seat until they are big enough to fit in a seat belt properly. For a seat belt to fit properly, the lap belt must lie snugly across the upper thighs, not the stomach. The shoulder belt should lie snugly across the shoulder and chest. It should not cross the neck or face. *Remember:* The child should still ride in the back seat because it's safer there.		
13 years and older A seat belt should lie across the upper thighs and be snug across the shoulder and chest to restrain the child safely in a crash. It should not rest on the stomach area or across the neck.		
Car safety: preventing injury		
1. Everyone who rides in a car should wear a seat belt.		
2. All children younger than 13 years should ride in the back seat.		
3. Everyone should keep their arms and legs inside the car.		
4. Never leave children alone in or around cars, even for a minute.		
5. Make sure all child passengers have left the vehicle after it is parked.		

(continued)

Action	I follow this safety precaution	Purchase of safety item is required
6. Take action to make sure you never leave a child in the car. • Put something you'll need, like your cell phone, handbag, employee ID, or briefcase, on the floorboard in the back seat. This will cause you to always look in the back seat before locking the car. • Keep a large stuffed animal in the child's car seat when the child isn't sitting in it. When the child is placed in the seat, put the stuffed animal in the front passenger seat. This will remind you that anytime the stuffed animal is up front, the child is in the back seat in a child safety seat. • Alert your child's day care center or babysitter that you will always phone if your child is not going to be there as scheduled.		
7. Keep vehicles locked at all times, even in the garage or driveway. Always set your parking brake.		
8. Do not leave keys and remote openers within reach of children.		
9. Children should cross streets at cross walks. Teach them street-crossing safety.		
10. Children should hold hands with or be carried by an adult in a parking lot or other places where cars are moving and drivers might not see a child walking.		
Preparation for first aid emergencies		
11. Make sure emergency phone numbers are easy to find. Place a sticker or card with these numbers near or on a landline phone; program the numbers into your cell phone. Important numbers include police, fire department, poison control center, hospital emergency services, and healthcare providers. Also include your address and phone number.		
12. Make sure that the building number can be seen from the street. This is so that EMS providers can find it without delay.		
13. Maintain a fully stocked first aid kit. Know where it is located.		
14. Schools and childcare facilities should have a health record and written first aid action plan for each child with a medical condition.		
Kitchen safety: preventing burns and other injury		
15. To reduce the risk of burns • Keep hot liquids, foods, and cooking utensils out of a child's reach. • Place hot liquids and food away from the edge of the table. • Cook on back burners when possible. Turn pot handles toward the center of the stove (away from the front and edges of the stove). • Avoid using tablecloths and placemats that can be pulled, spilling hot liquids or food. • Keep high chairs and stools away from the stove. • Do not keep snacks near the stove. • Do not hold a child or infant while cooking or carrying hot foods or liquids.		
16. Keep knives and other sharp objects out of a child's reach.		

(continued)

Action	I follow this safety precaution	Purchase of safety item is required
Bathroom safety: preventing injury		
17. Bathe children in no more than 1 or 2 inches of water. Stay with young children and infants throughout bath time. Do not leave small infants or toddlers in the bathtub in the care of young siblings.		
18. Use skidproof mats or stickers in the bathtub. Put a cushioned cover over faucets.		
19. Adjust the maximum temperature of the water heater to 120 degrees Fahrenheit (48.9 degrees Celsius) or below. Test the temperature with a thermometer.		
20. Keep electrical appliances out of the bathroom or unplugged. Keep them away from water and out of a child's reach. This includes radios, hair dryers, and space heaters.		
Indoor safety: preventing fire injury		
21. Install smoke detectors in the hallway outside areas where children sleep or nap. Install them on each floor at the head of stairs. Test the alarm each month. Replace batteries once a year. (A good reminder is to replace batteries in the fall when the time changes from daylight saving time.)		
22. Install carbon monoxide detectors. Test them each month.		
23. Make sure that there is an emergency exit from the home, childcare center, classroom, or other area where children are likely to be present. Two exits are preferred. Make sure nothing is blocking the exit(s).		
24. Develop and practice a fire escape plan.		
25. Make sure that a working fire extinguisher is available. This is especially important in areas that have the greatest risk of fire. Some of these areas are the kitchen, furnace room, and near the fireplace.		
26. Make sure that all space heaters are safety approved and in safe operating condition. Place heaters out of a child's reach. They should be at least 3 feet from curtains, papers, and furniture. Heaters should have protective covers.		
27. Make sure all wood-burning stoves and fireplaces are inspected yearly and vented properly. Place stoves out of a child's reach.		
28. Make sure that electrical cords are not frayed or overloaded. Place out of a child's reach.		
29. Keep matches and lighters up high, out of children's sight and reach.		
30. Supervise children if a live candle is in the room. Blow out all candles when you leave the room or go to bed. Avoid the use of candles in the bedroom and other areas where people may fall asleep.		
31. Have flashlights and battery-powered lighting to use during a power outage.		
Indoor safety: preventing electrical injury		
32. Install plastic outlet plugs or outlet covers on all electrical outlets.		

(continued)

Action	I follow this safety precaution	Purchase of safety item is required
33. Make sure cords are not frayed or cracked. Keep cords out of reach of children.		
34. Make sure plugs fit properly into the outlets.		
Indoor safety: preventing falls		
35. Always keep one hand on an infant sitting or lying on a high surface, such as a changing table. Never leave an infant alone on a changing table, couch, bed, or other furniture.		
36. If the infant is in a carrier, place it on the floor rather than on a table, sofa, or bed.		
37. Keep halls and stairs lighted to prevent falls.		
38. Put baby gates at the top and bottom of stairs. (Do not use accordion-type gates with wide spaces at the top. The child's head could become trapped in such a gate. The child could strangle.)		
39. Infants and children should use stationary activity centers. Avoid infant walkers because they can lead to injuries.		
40. Install window guards to keep windows from opening completely.		
Indoor safety: preventing SIDS		
41. Place healthy full-term infants on their backs on a firm mattress to sleep.		
42. Make sure the crib is safe: • The crib mattress should fit snugly, with no more than 2 fingers' width between the mattress and crib railing. • The distance between crib slats should be no more than 2⅜ inches (so the infant's head won't be caught). • Keep all loose blankets, toys, and other items out of the bed. • Keep hanging crib toys out of reach.		
43. Use a crib in good repair. Avoid portable bed rails.		
44. Check to see if the crib or mattress has been recalled.		
45. Infants need their own infant beds. The American Academy of Pediatrics does not recommend any bed-sharing arrangements as safe.		
Indoor safety: preventing poisoning		
46. Store medicines and vitamins in child-resistant containers out of a child's reach. Lock drawers and cabinets.		
47. Store cleaning products out of a child's sight and reach. • Store and label all household poisons in their original containers in high, locked cabinets (not under sinks). • Do not store chemicals or poisons in soda bottles. • Store cleaning products away from food.		

(continued)

Action	I follow this safety precaution	Purchase of safety item is required
48. Install safety latches or locks on cabinets that are within a child's reach and contain possible dangerous items.		
49. Keep purses that contain dangerous items out of a child's reach. Some of these items are vitamins, medicines, cigarettes, and matches. Others are jewelry and calculators. These may have easy-to-swallow button batteries.		
50. Install a lock or hook-and-eye latch on the door to the basement or garage to keep children from entering those areas. Put a lock at the top of the doorframe.		
51. Keep plants that may be harmful out of a child's reach. (Many plants are poisonous. Check with your poison control center.)		
Indoor safety: other prevention actions		
52. Tie up blind and window curtain cords.		
Preventing choking		
53. Keep all small items (including food items) that can choke a child out of reach. Test toys for size with a toilet paper roll. If the toy can fit inside the roll, it can choke a child.		
Toy safety		
54. Make sure that toy chests have lightweight lids, no lids, or safe-closing hinges.		
55. Follow age recommendations on toy labels.		
Outdoor safety: playground		
56. Make sure playground equipment is assembled and anchored correctly according to the manufacturer's instructions. The playground should have a level, cushioned surface, such as sand or wood chips.		
57. Remove any broken glass or trash from playground areas.		
58. Protect children from heat- or cold-related injuries in very hot or cold weather.		
Outdoor safety: bikes, skateboards, fireworks		
59. Make sure your child knows the rules of safe bicycling: • Wear a protective helmet. • Use the correct-size bicycle. • Ride on the right side of the road (with traffic). • Use hand signals. • Wear bright or reflective clothing. • Never bicycle in the dark or fog. • Young children riding alone should only bike on sidewalks or paths.		

(continued)

Action	I follow this safety precaution	Purchase of safety item is required
60. Make sure your child is properly protected while roller skating or skateboarding: • Wear a helmet and protective pads on the knees and elbows. • Skate only in rinks or parks that are free of traffic.		
61. Do not allow children to play with fireworks.		
Outdoor safety: sports		
62. Make sure your child is properly protected while participating in contact sports: • Children should have proper instruction and adult supervision. • Children should wear appropriate safety equipment, such as mouth guards and helmets.		
63. Before a child starts to play a new organized sport, the parents or caregivers should check with a healthcare provider to • Ensure that the child is healthy enough to play the sport • Identify any health issues that might put the child at risk for illness or injury		
Outdoor safety: preventing bites and stings		
64. To reduce the risk of animal bites, teach children the following: • How to handle and care for a pet • To avoid unfamiliar animals • To approach dogs calmly and slowly • To check with the owner first before approaching or petting		
65. To reduce the risk of insect bites and stings, do the following: • Keep children from bothering insects. • Use insect repellent that is approved for use on children. • If you know a child has a severe allergy to an insect bite or bee sting, keep their epinephrine pen close by at all times, especially when the child is outdoors. • Have children wear light-colored clothing that covers the arms and legs when walking or playing in areas where insects are likely to be. • Keep flowering plants and gardens away from areas where children play. • Put outdoor toys away so spiders and insects can't hide inside them.		
Outdoor safety: preventing drowning		
66. An adult must always supervise children while they swim. Never allow a child to swim alone.		
67. Closely watch children around any body of water.		
68. Children should wear life jackets in boats and at other times as needed.		
69. Pools and nearby properties should be protected from use by unsupervised children.		
70. Empty and turn over wading pools as soon as children are done using them.		

(continued)

Action	I follow this safety precaution	Purchase of safety item is required
71. Do not leave a child alone around any water. A small child or an infant can drown if they fall in a bucket, toilet, or other container filled with water.		
72. If you have a home swimming pool, make sure of the following: • The pool is totally enclosed with fencing. • Fencing is at least 4 feet high. • All gates are self-closing and self-latching. • There is no direct access (without passing through a locked gate) from the home into the pool area.		
73. All adults and older children should learn CPR.		
Outdoor safety: preventing sunburn		
74. Protect children from sunburns: • Keep infants younger than 6 months out of direct sunlight. • For children older than 6 months, use sunscreen made for children. • Put sunscreen on children 30 minutes before they go outside. • Choose a water-resistant or waterproof sunscreen that blocks both ultraviolet A and ultraviolet B rays and has an SPF of at least 15. • Reapply waterproof sunscreen every 2 hours, especially if children are playing in the water. • Try to stay out of the sun between 10 AM and 4 PM.		
Firearms: preventing injuries		
75. If firearms are stored in the home, keep them locked. They should be out of a child's sight and reach. Lock and unload each gun before storing it. Store ammunition separate from the firearms.		

The following sources were used in compiling the checklist:

- National Highway Traffic Safety Administration
- Centers for Disease Control and Prevention
- American Academy of Pediatrics
- Safe Kids USA
- KidsAndCars.org
- National Institutes of Health Medline Plus (Gun Safety)
- National Fire Protection Association

Preventing Illness and Injury: Review Questions

1. To help protect a child from burns, you should
    a. Keep hot appliances, like irons or curling irons, out of children's reach
    b. Keep children away from hot liquids, such as a cup of coffee
    c. Cook on the back burners, and keep children away from the stove
    d. All of the above

2. Which of the following reduces the risk of SIDS?
    a. Putting the infant to sleep on their back
    b. Putting the infant to sleep on their stomach
    c. Ensuring that the infant has a first aid action plan
    d. Ensuring that the infant's car seat is installed correctly

3. A correctly installed car seat will not shift side to side or back to front more than
    a. 1 inch
    b. 1½ inches
    c. 2 inches
    d. 2½ inches

4. In a poisoning emergency, whom should you call first?
    a. An urgent care center
    b. The poison control center
    c. 9-1-1
    d. The child's parent or caregiver

5. Before a child starts playing an organized sport, the parent or caregiver should
    a. Have their abilities assessed to see if they will be good at the sport
    b. Do nothing—just show up on the first day, ready to play
    c. Check with the child's healthcare provider to identify any illness or injury that might put the child at risk
    d. Wait until the child has played the sport for several weeks to see if any problems develop

6. If a child has a known allergy to bee stings, you should
    a. Not allow the child to participate in outdoor activities
    b. Make sure that the child's epinephrine pen is available at all times
    c. Keep the child inside except during the winter
    d. Call the parent or caregiver if the child gets stung before you do anything else

7. Which of the following can cause a poisoning emergency?

   a. A button battery

   b. A dishwasher tablet

   c. Blood pressure pills from grandmother's purse

   d. All of the above

Answers: 1. d, 2. a, 3. a, 4. c, 5. c, 6. b, 7. d

Part 5: First Aid Resources

Topics covered in this Part are

- Sample first aid kit
- Sample first aid action plan
- How children act and tips for interacting with them
- Child abuse and neglect
- Preventing the spread of contagious diseases

Sample First Aid Kit

First Aid Kit Maintenance

One responsibility of a first aid provider is to maintain the first aid kit. The kit should always contain the supplies you'll need for most common emergencies.

Table 3 is a sample list of contents for a first aid kit. The list divides recommended first aid kit supplies into 2 categories: Class A and Class B. Class A kits are suitable for homes or smaller workplaces. Class B kits are for larger workplaces and are designed to treat injuries more often found in densely populated workplaces with complex or high-risk environments, such as warehouses, factories, and outdoor areas. Use your best judgment on which class is most suitable for your location, and always be sure to restock the kit after any emergency. These lists follow the standards of the American National Standards Institute (ANSI); you can find more information at **ansi.org**.

Table 3. Sample First Aid Kit List

First aid supply	Minimum quantity		Minimum size or volume	
	Class A kits	Class B kits	US	Metric
Adhesive bandage	16	50	1 × 3 in	2.5 × 7.5 cm
Adhesive tape	1	2	2.5 yd (total)	2.3 m
Antibiotic application	10	25	1/57 oz	0.5 g
Antiseptic	10	50	1/57 oz	0.5 g
Breathing barrier	1	1	N/A	N/A
Burn dressing (gel soaked)	1	2	4 × 4 in	10 × 10 cm
Burn treatment	10	25	1/32 oz	0.9 g
Cold pack	1	2	4 × 5 in	10 × 12.5 cm
Eye covering (with means of attachment)	2	2	2.9 sq in	19 sq cm
Eye/skin wash	1 fl oz total			29.6 mL
		4 fl oz total		118.3 mL
Hand sanitizer	6	10	1/32 oz	0.9 g
Medical exam gloves	2 pair	4 pair	N/A	N/A
Roller bandage (2 inch)	1	2	2 in × 4 yd	5 cm × 3.66 m
Roller bandage (4 inch)	0	1	4 in × 4 yd	10 cm × 3.66 m
Scissors	1	1	N/A	N/A
Splint	0	1	4.0 × 24 in	10.2 × 61 cm
Sterile pad	2	4	3 × 3 in	7.5 × 7.5 cm
Tourniquet	0	1	1 in (width)	2.5 cm (width)
Trauma pad	2	4	5 × 9 in	12.7 × 22.9 cm
Triangular bandage	1	2	40 × 40 × 56 in	101 × 101 × 142 cm
Directions for requesting emergency assistance (including a list of important local emergency telephone numbers, such as the police, fire department, EMS, and poison control center*)	1	1	N/A	N/A
Heartsaver First Aid Digital Reference Guide*	1	1	N/A	N/A

*Items marked with an asterisk are in addition to those listed in the ANSI guidelines.

Sample First Aid Action Plan

This is a sample only. The actions listed are not for use for an actual child. Always follow instructions from the child's caregiver or physician.

Seizure First Aid Action Plan for
Jimmy Childs

Date of Birth: June 3, 2009
Parents: John and Mary Childs
Parents' Contact Phone Number: 999-452-5555 or 999-321-4444
Jimmy's Physician (for seizures): Dr. AJ Nest, 999-322-3333

Medical Condition: Seizures

Jimmy Childs has a condition known as *epilepsy.* He may have a seizure that will cause him to no longer respond and to have uncontrolled movements of his arms and legs. These seizures usually last a short time. These seizures may last for a longer time or occur with one followed quickly by another. Jimmy's seizures are usually controlled by his medicines, so seizures are unlikely but possible.

Possible triggers:

Bright, flashing lights may trigger seizure.

Staff members trained to give medicines:

1. Jean Oro
2. Martha Garcia

Staff members trained in First Aid and CPR AED:

1. Jean Oro
2. Martha Garcia
3. Jan Door
4. Stephen Glass

Actions:

Follow first aid actions for seizures as you have been trained to do.

If a seizure lasts longer than 4 minutes or if Jimmy has one seizure followed soon after by another, follow these actions. Only give medicines if you are one of the staff members trained to do so.

1. Have one staff member phone 9-1-1. Let them know a trained staff member will be giving rectal medicine prescribed by Jimmy's physician.
2. The trained staff member will get Jimmy medicine from the office cabinet. Have another staff member quickly check the label to verify that it is Jimmy's medicine.
3. If Jimmy is still having a seizure, give 1 dose of diazepam rectal gel using the steps printed on the package. (Protect Jimmy's privacy by using screens or moving his classmates out of sight.)
4. As soon as possible, contact John or Mary Childs.
5. A first aid–trained staff member will stay with Jimmy at all times.
6. If John or Mary Childs does not arrive by the time the ambulance is ready to transport Jimmy, instruct the emergency providers to take Jimmy to Oceanview Children's Hospital.

After Jimmy is in the care of emergency providers, write a summary. Include what happened before the seizure and during the seizure. Also include what happened after the medicine was given and after the seizure stopped. Provide a copy of this to John and Mary Childs.

How Children Act and Tips for Interacting With Them

Children who are ill, injured, or afraid often do not act their age in years. Instead, they may act like a younger child. Respond to ill, injured, or frightened children on the basis of their behavior, not their age.

Table 4 explains the characteristics and interaction tips for children of different ages.

Table 4. Characteristics and Interaction Tips for Children of Different Ages

Category	Age	Characteristics	Interaction tips

Infants	Birth to 1 year	• If younger than 4 months, may not be able to hold their heads up
		• Cannot talk
		• Will cry to tell you that they
		  – Are hungry
		  – Are tired
		  – Are wet
		  – Want to be held
		  – Are scared
		  – Are hurt or in pain
			• Support the head when you lift or carry an infant younger than 4 months.
			• Use a soft, quiet voice when you talk to an infant.
			• Use gentle motions when you approach an infant.
			• Keep the infant warm but not too hot.

Toddlers	1 to 3 years	• Learning to talk
		• Active, moving around and making noise
		• May bite other children when frustrated
		• If not active or acting differently than usual, they may be
		  – Ill
		  – Injured
		  – Afraid
		  – Tired
			• Toddlers may not speak well themselves.
			• They often can understand what others say.
			• They may be afraid of adults they do not know.
			• You may need to give extra comfort when a healthcare provider arrives to care for a toddler.

Young children	4 to 10 years	• Developmental stages overlap greatly within this age group • Often pick up on the verbal as well as nonverbal behavior of adults around them • Can understand simple explanations • Fear separation from caregivers and friends	• Stay calm. • Use simple words to tell young children what is happening. Be as truthful as possible. Do not lie to the child.

(continued)

Category	Age	Characteristics	Interaction tips

Adolescents	11 to 18 years	• Understand almost everything around them
		• Often act without worrying about consequences of their actions
		• May take risks, such as experimenting with drugs, drinking alcohol, and driving cars
		• May worry about
		  – How others view them
		  – Whether an injury will be permanent
		  – Getting into trouble because of an injury
		• May not share information with a first aid rescuer and especially their own parent or caregiver
			• Tell them what you are doing to help them.
			• Reassure them.
			• Don't disregard the child's complaints and concerns. Make it clear that you are listening carefully.

Children with special needs	Any age	• Have physical, mental, or emotional needs that require special care	Work with family members or other caregivers to know how to • Use medical devices or medicines • Discuss things with the child

Child Abuse and Neglect

Children of any age can suffer abuse and neglect. Abuse can be caused by parents, caregivers, or others who have a role in caring for the child.

Child abuse happens in every race, ethnicity, and class. The effects of abuse can last a lifetime.

Common Types of Abuse

There are 4 common types of abuse:

- Physical abuse: use of physical force, such as hitting, kicking, or shaking
- Sexual abuse: engaging a child in sexual acts or exposing a child to other sexual activities
- Emotional abuse: behaviors that harm a child's emotional well-being, such as shaming or name calling
- Neglect: failure to meet a child's basic needs, such as housing, food, or access to medicine

Shaken Baby Syndrome

Shaken baby syndrome is a kind of abuse. It happens when someone forcefully shakes an infant. It can severely injure the baby's eyes, neck, or brain. It can even cause death.

Suspect shaken baby syndrome if an infant has any of the following signs and you can't figure out why:

- Very sleepy or weak
- Very cranky
- Doesn't eat well
- Vomits for no reason
- Doesn't make sounds or smile
- Doesn't suck or swallow well
- Body gets stiff
- Has difficulty breathing

- Has seizures
- Can't lift their head
- Can't focus their eyes or follow movement

If you suspect an infant has suffered from shaken baby syndrome, phone 9-1-1.

Only suspect shaken baby syndrome if you can't explain why the infant has the sign. Sometimes infants are very cranky because they're ill or missed their nap.

Recognizing Possible Abuse

Children who have been abused may have marks or bruises. They may show signs of abuse in their behavior. Children usually can't or won't talk about the problem.

Sometimes children will tell someone they trust. Take these conversations seriously and report them.

You may suspect abuse if a child behaves in certain ways or has physical signs as noted in the following section.

Behavior Signs of Possible Abuse

A child who has been abused may behave in certain ways. Suspect abuse if the child

- Shows sudden changes in behavior or school performance
- Has unexplained learning problems (or difficulty concentrating)
- Is always watchful, as though preparing for something bad to happen
- Is overly compliant, passive, withdrawn
- Is very demanding and aggressive
- Comes to school or other activities early, stays late, and doesn't want to go home
- Is uncomfortable with physical contact
- Has low self-esteem
- Lags in physical, emotional, or intellectual development

Physical Signs of Possible Abuse

A child who has been abused may have physical signs. Suspect abuse if the injuries do not match the caregiver's explanation, including

- Bruises (especially bruises of differing ages and colors)
- Broken bones
- Burns
- Bleeding, cuts, punctures
- Bites
- Blood in the diaper or underwear
- Very low weight for the child's age
- Poor growth
- Trouble walking or sitting
- Untreated dental problems
- Headaches
- Stomachaches
- Poisoning
- Seizures
- Vomiting

To Report Abuse or Get Help

Reporting suspected abuse can help both the child and the family. If the abuse is not reported, the child will continue to be in danger. Sometimes child abuse can result in death.

In many states, anyone who suspects child abuse is required to report it. Phone the National Child Abuse Hotline at 1-800-4-A-CHILD (1-800-422-4453) to report a problem or to get help. All calls to this hotline are anonymous.

The identity of a person who reports child abuse is confidential. It can only be disclosed by court order or to a law enforcement officer involved in the investigation.

It's important to remember that the person who reports suspected abuse is responsible only for reporting the information. It's the role of law enforcement to determine if abuse is present.

To Learn More

To learn more about child abuse, see the following:

- Centers for Disease Control and Prevention: **cdc.gov/violenceprevention**
- Centers for Disease Control Facebook Page on Violence Prevention: **facebook.com/VetoViolence**
- Children's Bureau: **acf.hhs.gov/programs/cb**
- Child Welfare Information Gateway: **childwelfare.gov**
- FRIENDS National Center for Community-Based Child Abuse Prevention: **friendsnrc.org**

Sources

In addition to these links, the following sources also were used in compiling the abuse information:

- National Center on Shaken Baby Syndrome: **dontshake.org**
- About Shaken Baby: **aboutshakenbaby.com**
- Maryland and Oregon State Governments: **maryland.gov, oregon.gov**
- National Institutes of Health: **www.nlm.nih.gov/medlineplus/childabuse.html**
- Mayo Clinic: **mayoclinic.org**

Preventing the Spread of Contagious Diseases

Contagious diseases are a leading cause of illness and death in the United States. Vaccines are available that prevent these diseases. Good handwashing is essential to any disease prevention. Go to the following websites to learn more:

- **cdc.gov/vaccines**
- **vaccines.gov**
- **cdc.gov/flu/index.html**
- **cdc.gov/vaccinesafety/index.html**

This Part is a review of important first aid skills that you will have an opportunity to practice and demonstrate during the course. Topics covered in this Part are

- Removing protective gloves
- Finding the problem
- Controlling bleeding by direct pressure and bandaging
- Using an epinephrine pen
- Applying a splint

Summary

Remove Protective Gloves

Here is the correct way to remove protective gloves (Figure 29):

- Grip one glove on the outside near the cuff, and peel it down until it comes off inside out (Figure 29A).
- Cup it with your other gloved hand (Figure 29B).
- Place 2 fingers of your bare hand inside the cuff of the glove that is still on your other hand (Figure 29C).
- Peel that glove off so that it comes off inside out with the first glove inside it (Figure 29D).
- If blood or blood-containing material is on the gloves, dispose of the gloves properly.
  - Put the gloves in a biohazard waste bag.
  - If you don't have a biohazard waste bag, put the gloves in a plastic bag that can be sealed before you dispose of it.
- Always wash your hands after removing gloves, just in case some blood or body fluids came in contact with your hands.

Figure 29. Proper removal of protective gloves without touching the outside of the gloves.

A

B

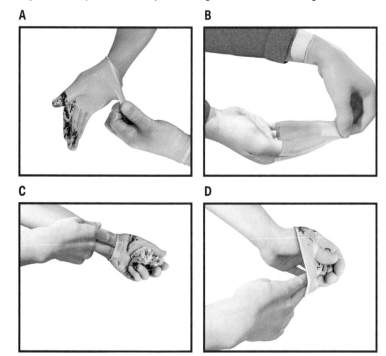

C

D

Find the Problem

Here are the steps for finding the problem. They are listed in order of importance, with the most important step listed first.

- Make sure the scene is safe.
- Check to see if the child responds. Approach the child, tap their shoulders, and shout, "Are you OK? Are you OK?"

If the child is responsive

- Ask what the problem is if the child is old enough to talk.
- If the child only moves, moans, or groans, shout for help.
- Phone or send someone to phone 9-1-1 and get the first aid kit and AED.
- Check the child's breathing.
  - If the child is breathing without difficulty and doesn't need immediate first aid, continue finding the problem.
  - If the child is having breathing problems, provide help. See Breathing Problems (Asthma) in Part 2.
- Check for any obvious signs of injury, such as bleeding, broken bones, burns, or bites.
- Look for any medical information jewelry that tells you if the child has a serious medical condition.
- Stay with the child until someone with more advanced training arrives and takes over.

If the child is unresponsive

- Shout for help and send someone to phone 9-1-1 and get a first aid kit and AED.
- Stay with the child.
  - If you are alone and no one comes to help and you have a cell phone, phone 9-1-1. Put the phone on speaker mode.
- Check for breathing.
  - If the child is breathing, roll them onto their side if you don't think they have a neck or back injury.
  - Phone 9-1-1 if no one has already done so. Stay with the child until advanced help arrives.
  - If the child is not breathing or is only gasping, perform 2 minutes of CPR.
  - Then, if no one has done so, phone 9-1-1 and get an AED (see Part 7: CPR and AED).
- Check for any obvious signs of injury, such as bleeding, broken bones, burns, or bites.
- Look for any medical information jewelry that tells you if the child has a serious medical condition.
- Stay with the child until someone with more advanced training arrives and takes over.

Control Bleeding by Direct Pressure and Bandaging

Here are the steps to stop bleeding:

- Apply dressings from the first aid kit. Put direct pressure on the dressings over the bleeding area. Use the flat part of your fingers or the palm of your hand (Figure 30).
- If the bleeding doesn't stop, you'll need to add more dressings and press harder. Do not remove a dressing once it's in place because this could cause the wound to bleed more. Keep pressure on the wound until it stops bleeding.
- For minor cuts and scrapes, wash the area with soap and water once the bleeding has stopped. Then, apply a dressing to the wound.
- Once the bleeding has stopped or if you can't keep pressure on the wound, wrap a bandage firmly over the dressings to hold them in place.

Figure 30. Controlling bleeding. **A,** A dressing can be a gauze pad or pads. **B,** It can be any other clean piece of cloth. **C,** If you don't have a dressing, use your gloved hand.

A

B

C

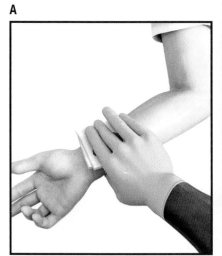
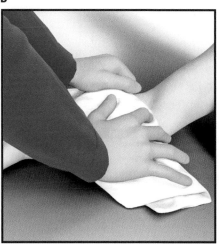

Use an Epinephrine Pen

Here are the steps to help someone who has signs of a severe allergic reaction use their epinephrine pen:

- Take off the safety cap (Figure 31A).
- Follow the instructions on the pen. Make sure you're holding the pen in your fist without touching either end because the needle comes out of one end. You may give the injection through clothes or on bare skin.
- Hold the leg firmly in place just before and during the injection. Press the tip of the injector hard against the side of the child's thigh, about halfway between the hip and the knee (Figure 31B).
  - Different injectors need to be held in place for different amounts of time. Be familiar with the manufacturer's instructions for the type of injector you are using. For example, EpiPen and EpiPen Jr injectors recommend holding the injector in place for 3 seconds. Some other injectors recommend holding them in place for up to 10 seconds.
- Pull the pen straight out, making sure that you don't touch the end that was pressed against the child's thigh.
- Either the person getting the injection or the person giving the injection should rub the injection spot for about 10 seconds.
- Note the time of the injection.
- If the child doesn't get better, phone 9-1-1. If it takes more than 10 minutes for advanced help to arrive, consider giving a second dose, if available.
- Give any used pens to the emergency responders for proper disposal.

Figure 31. Using an epinephrine pen. **A,** Take off the safety cap. **B,** Press the tip of the injector hard against the side of the child's thigh, about halfway between the hip and the knee.

A

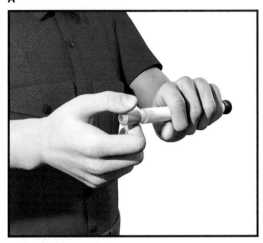

B

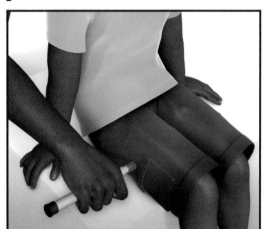

Assemble and Use an Inhaler

Here are the steps to assemble and use an inhaler:

- First, shake the medicine.
- Put the medicine canister into the mouthpiece.
- Remove the cap from the mouthpiece.
- Attach a spacer if there is one available and if you know how.

To help a child use an inhaler, ask the child to do the following:

- Tilt their head back slightly and breathe out slowly.
- Place the inhaler or spacer in their mouth.
- Push down on the medicine canister.
- Breathe in very deeply and slowly.
- Hold their breath for about 10 seconds.
- Then, breathe out slowly.

Apply a Splint

Here are the steps to apply a splint:

- Find an object that you can use to keep the injured arm or leg from moving.
  - Rolled-up towels, magazines, and pieces of wood can be used as splints. Splint in a way to reduce pain and limit further injury. The splint should be longer than the injured area. It should support the joints above and below the injury.
- After covering any broken skin with a clean or sterile cloth, tie or tape the splint to the injured limb so that it supports the injured area.
- Use tape, gauze, or cloth to secure it. It should fit snugly but not cut off circulation.
- If you're using a hard splint, like wood, make sure you pad it with something soft, like clothing or a towel.
- Keep the limb still until the injured child can be seen by a healthcare provider.

Prevention Strategies

Risks of Smoking and Vaping

The relationship between smoking and lung cancer is well known. But many don't know that smoking is also linked to heart disease, stroke, and other chronic diseases. Smoking can increase your risk for cancer of the bladder, throat, mouth, kidneys, cervix, and pancreas. Let's look at the facts:

- Smoking is a leading preventable cause of death in the United States and globally.
  - About 1 in 5 deaths from heart disease are due to smoking.
  - Smoking is linked to 80% to 90% of lung cancer deaths in the United States.
- Nicotine is a dangerous and highly addictive chemical.
  - It can cause an increase in blood pressure, heart rate, and flow of blood to the heart as well as a narrowing of the arteries or vessels that carry blood.
  - Nicotine may also contribute to the hardening of the arterial walls, which may lead to a heart attack.
  - This chemical can stay in your body for 6 to 8 hours, depending on how often you smoke. Also, as with most addictive substances, there are some side effects of withdrawal.

Today, we are exposed to cigars, cigarillos, e-cigarettes (which can be used for vaping and using a JUUL cartridge), hookah (a type of water pipe), and smokeless tobacco (such as snuff, chew, and dissolvable tobacco). Several of these forms of tobacco are flavored, increasing their appeal, especially to young people. All tobacco products, including smokeless tobacco, hookah, and e-cigarettes, have dangers, including nicotine addiction. Many people falsely believe that e-cigarettes are safe. Some don't even realize they contain nicotine. But they can deliver much higher concentrations of addictive nicotine than traditional cigarettes can.

The bottom line is that tobacco products contain many dangerous toxins. The best thing you can do for your health is to quit tobacco entirely.

You can find resources to help you quit using tobacco products at **heart.org/tobacco**.

Benefits of a Healthy Lifestyle

Add Color

Fruits and vegetables provide many beneficial nutrients, including vitamins, minerals, healthy fats, protein, calcium, fiber, antioxidants, and phytonutrients.

On their own, fruits and vegetables typically contain no trans fat, low saturated fat, and very little or no sodium. The natural sugars they contain don't affect your health the same way added sugars do.

Fruits and vegetables also tend to be low in calories, so they can help you manage your weight while still filling you up—thanks to the fiber and water they contain. Replacing higher-calorie foods with fruits and vegetables is an easy first step to a healthier eating plan.

All forms of fruits and vegetables (fresh, frozen, canned, dried, and 100% juice) can be part of a healthy diet. They can be eaten raw or cooked, whole or chopped, organic or not, and alone or in combination with other foods. They are among the most versatile, convenient, and affordable foods you can eat.

A healthy eating plan rich in fruits and vegetables can help lower your risk of many serious and chronic health conditions, including heart disease, stroke, obesity, high blood pressure, high blood cholesterol, diabetes, kidney disease, osteoporosis, and some types of cancer. They're also essential to many daily functions of a healthy body. An easy first step to eating healthy is to include fruits and vegetables at every meal and snack.

To learn more about adding color to your diet, visit **heart.org/addcolor**.

Move More

Here are some tools and tips to get you on the right path to a healthier lifestyle:

- **Just move more!** There are lots of fun and easy ways to build more activity into your everyday routine, even if you're not a gym hero.
- **Set a goal.** Having a commitment or goal, like being active for at least 150 minutes each week, will help you stay on track. Share it with others to keep yourself accountable. If you're the competitive type, challenge friends or family to see who can consistently meet their goals over time.
- **Put fitness first.** Shake up your evening routine. Go for a bike ride or shoot some hoops when you get home from work or school. You'll feel better and think better!
- **Put the screens on hold.** Instead of heading right for the TV or game console after dinner, take a walk or practice a sport.
- **Do what you love.** Find activities that fit your personality and motivate you to stick with them. If you're a social person, try a group dance class or a kickball team, or walk with a group of friends. If you prefer time alone, yoga or running might be a better fit.

For more information, including resources to help you get active, visit **heart.org/movemore**.

Part 7: CPR and AED

Although much is being done to prevent death from heart problems, cardiac arrest is still one of the leading causes of death in the United States. And about 70% of the arrests that happen outside of the hospital happen at home.

In this Part, you'll learn skills that will help you to recognize cardiac arrest, get emergency care on the way quickly, and help the person until more advanced care arrives to take over.

CPR AED Course Objectives

At the end of the CPR AED portion of this course, you will be able to

- Describe how high-quality CPR improves survival
- Explain the concepts of the Chain of Survival
- Recognize when someone needs CPR
- Perform high-quality CPR for all age groups
- Describe how to perform CPR with help from others
- Give effective breaths by using mouth-to-mouth or a mask for all age groups
- Demonstrate how to use an AED on children and adults
- Describe when and how to help someone who is choking

Difference Between Cardiac Arrest and Heart Attack

People often use the terms *cardiac arrest* and *heart attack* to mean the same thing—but they're not the same. Cardiac arrest is a "rhythm" problem. It happens when the heart malfunctions and stops beating unexpectedly. A heart attack is a "clot" problem. It happens when a clot blocks blood flow.

Cardiac Arrest

Cardiac arrest results from an abnormal heart rhythm. This abnormal rhythm causes the heart to quiver so that it can no longer pump blood to the brain, lungs, and other organs. Within seconds, the person becomes unresponsive and is not breathing or is only gasping. Death happens within minutes if the person does not receive immediate lifesaving treatment.

Heart Attack

A heart attack happens when blood flow to part of the heart muscle is blocked by a clot. Typically during a heart attack, the heart continues to pump blood. A person having a heart attack may have discomfort or pain in the chest. There may be an uncomfortable feeling in one or both arms, the neck, the jaw, or the upper back.

The longer the person with a heart attack goes without treatment, the greater the possible damage to the heart muscle. Occasionally, the damaged heart muscle triggers an abnormal rhythm that can lead to cardiac arrest.

CPR and AED Use for Children

In this section, you'll learn when CPR is needed, how to give CPR to a child, and how to use an AED.

Definition of a Child

For the purposes of this course, a child is from 1 year of age to puberty. Signs of puberty include chest or underarm hair on boys and any breast development for girls. If you are not sure whether someone is an adult or child, provide emergency care as if the person is an adult. But note that the definition of *child* is different when using an AED compared with providing CPR (see Use an AED later in this section).

Pediatric Chain of Survival

The AHA pediatric Chain of Survival (Figure 32) shows the most important actions needed to treat children who have cardiac arrests outside of a hospital. During this course, you will learn about the first 3 links of the chain. The fourth and fifth links are advanced care provided by emergency responders and hospital providers who will take over care, and the sixth link is recovery.

Remember that seconds count when a child has a cardiac arrest. Wherever you are, take action. The pediatric Chain of Survival starts with you!

- **First link:** Preventing injury and cardiac arrest is an important first step in saving children's lives.
- **Second link:** Phoning 9-1-1 as soon as possible so that the child can have emergency care quickly improves outcome.
- **Third link:** The sooner that high-quality CPR is started for someone in cardiac arrest, the better the chances of survival.
- **Fourth and fifth links:** Advanced care is provided.
- **Sixth link:** A child may need continued care and support for months or years to fully recover after a cardiac arrest.

Figure 32. The AHA pediatric Chain of Survival for cardiac arrests that happen outside of a hospital.

Respiratory Problems Often Cause Cardiac Arrest in Children

Children usually have healthy hearts, and breathing trouble is often the cause of a child needing CPR. In the pediatric Chain of Survival, preventing cardiac arrest is one of the most important things you can do. This includes prevention of drowning, choking, and other respiratory problems.

Because respiratory problems are often the cause of cardiac arrest in children, if you are alone and don't have a phone nearby, provide CPR for 2 minutes (5 sets of compressions and breaths) before leaving to phone 9-1-1.

Topics covered in this section are

- Assessing and phoning 9-1-1
- Performing high-quality CPR
- Using an AED
- Putting it all together: child high-quality CPR AED summary

Assess and Phone 9-1-1

When you encounter a child who may have had a cardiac arrest, take the following 5 steps to assess the emergency and get help:

1. Make sure the scene is safe.
2. Tap and shout (check for responsiveness).
3. Shout for help.
4. Check for breathing.
5. Phone 9-1-1, begin CPR, and get an AED.

Depending on the circumstance and the resources you have available, you may be able to perform some of these actions at the same time. You might, for example, phone 9-1-1 with your cell phone on speaker mode while checking for breathing.

Step 1: Make Sure the Scene Is Safe

Before you begin to help the child, look for anything nearby that might hurt you. You can't help if you get hurt too.

Some places that may be unsafe are

- A busy street or parking lot
- An area where power lines are down
- A room with poisonous fumes

As you help, be aware if anything changes and makes it unsafe for you or the child.

Step 2: Tap and Shout (Check for Responsiveness)

Tap and shout to check if the child is responsive or unresponsive (Figure 33). Lean over the child or kneel at their side. Tap their shoulders and ask if they're OK.

- If they move, speak, blink, or otherwise react when you tap their shoulders, they're responsive. Ask if they need help.
- If they don't move, speak, blink, or otherwise react when you tap their shoulders, they're unresponsive. Shout for help so that if others are nearby, they can help you.

Figure 33. Tap and shout (check for responsiveness).

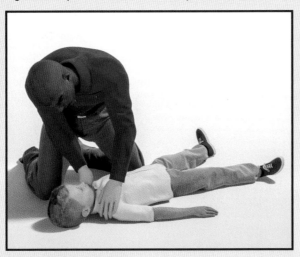

Step 3: Shout for Help

In an emergency, the sooner you realize that there's a problem and get help, the better it is for the child with a cardiac arrest. When more people are helping, you can provide better care.

If the child is unresponsive, shout for help (Figure 34). If someone comes, send that person to phone 9-1-1 and get an AED. If you have a cell phone, phone 9-1-1 and put it on speaker mode.

Figure 34. Shout for help.

Step 4: Check for Breathing

If the child is unresponsive, check for breathing (Figure 35).

Scan the chest repeatedly for at least 5 seconds, but no more than 10 seconds, looking for chest rise and fall. If the child is not breathing or is only gasping, they need CPR. See Heartsaver Pediatric First Aid CPR AED Terms and Concepts for more information on gasping.

If the child is unresponsive and is breathing

- This child does not need CPR.
- Roll them onto their side (if you don't think they have a neck or back injury). This will help keep the airway clear in case the child vomits.
- If no one has done so, phone 9-1-1, and then return to the child.
- If the child is having breathing problems, help them. See Breathing Problems (Asthma) in Part 2.
- Stay with the child until advanced help arrives.

If the child is unresponsive and is not breathing or is only gasping

- This child needs CPR.
- Make sure the child is lying faceup on a firm, flat surface.
- Have someone phone 9-1-1, or use your cell phone (or nearby phone), put it on speaker mode, and phone 9-1-1.
- Begin CPR. Give 5 sets of 30 compressions and 2 breaths.
- After 5 sets of compressions and breaths, phone 9-1-1 and get an AED (if no one has done this yet).
- Use the AED as soon as it's available.
- Resume CPR and using the AED until advanced help arrives and takes over.

Remember: Unresponsive + No breathing or only gasping = Provide CPR

Figure 35. Check for breathing.

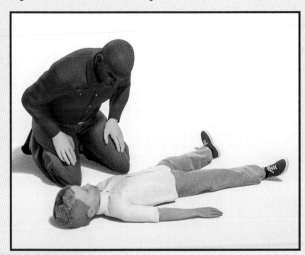

Step 5: Phone 9-1-1, Begin CPR, and Get an AED

- Make sure the child is lying faceup on a firm, flat surface.
- Have someone phone 9-1-1, or use your cell phone (or nearby phone), put it on speaker mode, and phone 9-1-1.
- Begin CPR. Give 5 sets of 30 compressions and 2 breaths.
- After 5 sets of compressions and breaths, phone 9-1-1 and get an AED (if no one has done this yet). Use the AED as soon as it's available.

If someone comes to help and a cell phone is available

- Ask the person to phone 9-1-1 on the cell phone, put it on speaker mode, and go get an AED while you begin CPR.
- Use the AED as soon as it is available.

If someone comes to help and a cell phone is not available

- Ask the person to go phone 9-1-1 and get an AED while you begin CPR.
- Use the AED as soon as it is available.

If you are alone and have a cell phone or a nearby phone

- Phone 9-1-1 and put the phone on speaker mode while you begin CPR.
- Give 5 sets of 30 compressions and 2 breaths.
- Go get an AED. Use it as soon as it is available.
- Return to the child and continue CPR.

If you are alone and don't have a cell phone

- Give 5 sets of 30 compressions and 2 breaths.
- Go phone 9-1-1 and get an AED. Use the AED as soon as it is available.
- Return to the child and continue CPR.
- Continue providing CPR and using the AED until
  - Someone else arrives who can take turns providing CPR with you
  - The child begins to move, speak, blink, or otherwise react
  - Someone with more advanced training arrives

Follow the Dispatcher's Instructions

Stay on the phone until the 9-1-1 dispatcher tells you to hang up. Answering the dispatcher's questions will not delay the arrival of help.

The dispatcher will ask you about the emergency—where you are and what has happened. Dispatchers can provide instructions that will help you, such as telling you how to provide CPR, use an AED, or give first aid.

That's why it's important to put the phone on speaker mode after phoning 9-1-1. It allows the dispatcher and the person providing CPR to speak to each other.

What to Do if You Are Not Sure

It's better to give CPR to a child who doesn't need it than not to give it to a child who does need it. CPR is not likely to cause harm if the child is not in cardiac arrest. But without CPR, a child who is in cardiac arrest may die.

So if you aren't sure, provide CPR. You may save a child's life.

Summary

Here is a summary of how to assess the emergency and get help when you encounter an ill or injured child:

Assess and Get Help

- Make sure the scene is safe.
- Tap and shout (check for responsiveness).
  - If the child is responsive, ask, "Do you need help?"
  - If the child is unresponsive, go to the next step.
- Shout for help.
- Check for breathing.
  - If the child is breathing, stay with the child until advanced help arrives.
  - If the child is not breathing or is only gasping, begin CPR and use an AED. See the next steps.

Phone 9-1-1, Begin CPR, and Get an AED

- Make sure the child is lying faceup on a firm, flat surface.
- Quickly move bulky clothes out of the way. If a child's clothes are difficult to remove, you can still provide compressions over clothing.
  - If an AED becomes available, remove all clothes that cover the chest. AED pads must not be placed over any clothing.
- Phone 9-1-1, begin CPR, and get an AED.

If someone comes to help and a cell phone is available

- Ask the person to phone 9-1-1 on the cell phone, put it on speaker mode, and go get an AED while you begin CPR.
- Use the AED as soon as it is available.

If someone comes to help and a cell phone is not available

- Ask the person to go phone 9-1-1 and get an AED while you begin CPR.
- Use the AED as soon as it is available.

If you are alone and have a cell phone or a nearby phone

- Phone 9-1-1 and put the phone on speaker mode while you begin CPR.
- Give 5 sets of 30 compressions and 2 breaths.
- Go get an AED, and use it as soon as it is available.
- Return to the child and continue CPR.

If you are alone and don't have a cell phone

- Give 5 sets of 30 compressions and 2 breaths.
- Go phone 9-1-1 and get an AED, and use it as soon as it is available.
- Return to the child and continue CPR.
- Continue providing CPR and using the AED until
  - Someone else arrives who can take turns providing CPR with you
  - The child begins to move, speak, blink, or otherwise react
  - Someone with more advanced training arrives

Perform High-Quality CPR

Learning how to perform high-quality CPR is important. The better you can perform CPR skills, the better the person's chances of survival.

CPR has 2 main skills: providing compressions and giving breaths. In this section, you'll learn how to perform these skills for a child in cardiac arrest. The AHA encourages bystanders who are not trained in CPR to give compression-only CPR, or Hands-Only CPR, if they see someone collapse. In the first few minutes of cardiac arrest, survival rates of those who have received Hands-Only CPR and those who have received CPR with breaths are similar. There are 2 simple steps to follow: phone 9-1-1, and push hard and fast in the center of the chest. If you are willing and able to give breaths, you should do so, especially for children or anyone who might be in cardiac arrest due to respiratory issues such as drowning or drug overdose.

Provide Compressions

A *compression* is the act of pushing hard and fast on the chest. When a child's heart stops, blood stops flowing through the body. When you push on the chest, you pump blood to the brain and other organs.

To perform high-quality compressions, make sure that you

- Provide compressions that are deep enough
- Provide compressions that are fast enough
- Let the chest come back up to its normal position after each compression
- Try not to interrupt compressions for more than 10 seconds, even when you give breaths

Compression depth is an important part of providing high-quality compressions. You need to push hard enough to pump blood through the body. It's better to push too hard than not hard enough. People are often afraid of injuring a child by providing compressions, but injury is unlikely.

Compression Technique

When providing compressions for a child, use 1 hand (Figure 36). If you can't push down at least one third the depth of the child's chest (or approximately 2 inches) with 1 hand, use 2 hands to compress the chest (Figure 37).

Here is how to provide compressions for a child during CPR:

- Make sure the child is lying faceup on a firm, flat surface.
- Quickly move bulky clothes out of the way. If a child's clothes are difficult to remove, you can still provide compressions over clothing.
  - If an AED becomes available, remove all clothes that cover the chest. AED pads must not be placed over any clothing.
- Use 1 or 2 hands to give compressions.
  - **1 hand:** Put the heel of one hand on the center of the child's chest, over the lower half of the breastbone.
  - **2 hands:** Put the heel of one hand on the center of the child's chest, over the lower half of the breastbone. Put your other hand on top of the first hand.
- Push straight down at least one third the depth of the chest, or approximately 2 inches.
- Push at a rate of 100 to 120/min. Count the compressions out loud.
- Let the chest come back up to its normal position after each compression.
- Try not to interrupt chest compressions for more than 10 seconds, even when you give breaths.

Figure 36. Using 1 hand to give compressions to a child.

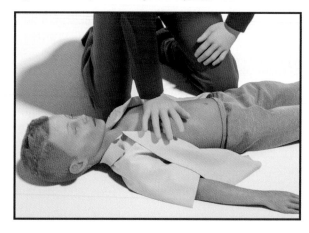

Figure 37. Using 2 hands to give compressions to a child.

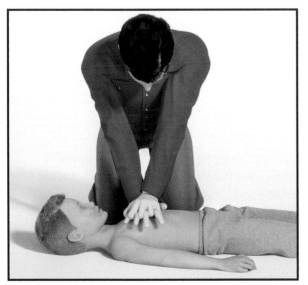

Switch Rescuers to Avoid Fatigue

Performing chest compressions correctly is hard work. The more tired you become, the less effective your compressions will be.

If someone else knows CPR, you can take turns providing compressions (Figure 38). Switch rescuers about every 2 minutes, or sooner if you get tired. Move quickly to keep any pauses in compressions as short as possible.

Remind other rescuers to perform high-quality CPR as described in this workbook.

Figure 38. Switch rescuers about every 2 minutes to avoid fatigue.

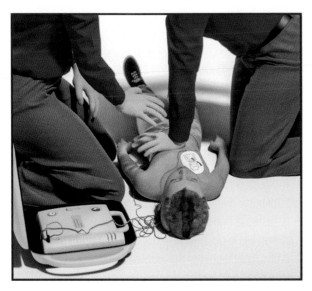

Give Breaths

The second skill of CPR is giving breaths. After each set of 30 compressions, you will need to give 2 breaths. Breaths may be given with or without a barrier device, such as a pocket mask or face shield.

When you give breaths, the breaths need to make the chest rise visibly. When you can see the chest rise, you know you have delivered an effective breath. For small children, you will not need to blow as much as for larger children.

Open the Airway

Before giving breaths, open the airway. This lifts the tongue from the back of the throat to make sure your breaths get air into the lungs.

Follow these steps to open the airway:
- Put one hand on the forehead and the fingers of your other hand on the bony part of the chin (Figure 39). Avoid pressing into the soft part of the neck or under the chin because this might block the airway.
- Tilt the head back and lift the chin.

Figure 39. Open the airway by tilting the head back and lifting the chin.

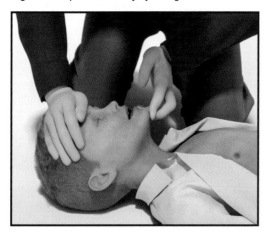

Pocket Masks for Giving Breaths

You can give breaths with or without a barrier device, such as a pocket mask. These plastic devices fit over the child's mouth and nose. They protect the rescuer from blood, vomit, or disease. Your instructor may discuss other types of barrier devices, like face shields, that you can use when giving breaths.

There are different kinds of pocket masks as well as different sizes. So make sure you're using the right size for a child. Pocket masks are typically made of hard plastic with a 1-way valve, which is the part you breathe into. You may need to put a pocket mask together before you use it.

Give Breaths Without a Pocket Mask

You may give breaths with or without a barrier device, such as a pocket mask. Giving someone breaths without a barrier device is usually quite safe. Use your best judgment on whether it's safe for you to give breaths without a barrier device.

Follow these steps to give breaths without a pocket mask or face shield:
- While holding the airway open, pinch the nose closed with your thumb and forefinger.
- Take a normal breath. Cover the child's mouth with your mouth (Figure 40).
- Give 2 breaths (blow for 1 second for each). Watch for the chest to begin to rise as you give each breath.
- Try not to interrupt chest compressions for more than 10 seconds, even when you give breaths.

Figure 40. Cover the child's mouth with your mouth.

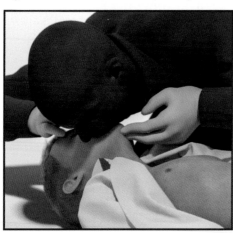

Give Breaths With a Pocket Mask

Follow these steps to give breaths with a pocket mask:
- Put the mask over the child's mouth and nose.
  - If the mask has a narrow, pointed end, put that end of the mask on the bridge of the nose; position the wide end so that it covers the mouth.
- Tilt the head and lift the chin while pressing the mask against the child's face. It is important to make an airtight seal between the child's face and the mask while you lift the chin to keep the airway open.
- Give 2 breaths (blow for 1 second for each). Watch for the chest to begin to rise as you give each breath (Figure 41).
- Try not to interrupt chest compressions for more than 10 seconds, even when you give breaths.

Figure 41. Giving breaths with a pocket mask.

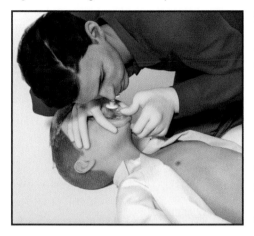

What to Do if the Chest Doesn't Rise

It takes a little practice to give breaths correctly. If you give someone a breath and the chest doesn't rise, do the following:

- Allow the head to go back to its normal position.
- Open the airway again by tilting the head back and lifting the chin.
- Then, give another breath. Make sure the chest rises.

Minimize Interruptions in Chest Compressions

If you have been unable to give 2 effective breaths in 10 seconds, go back to pushing hard and fast on the chest. Try to give breaths again after every 30 compressions. Don't interrupt compressions for more than 10 seconds.

Give Sets of 30 Compressions and 2 Breaths

When providing CPR, give sets of 30 compressions and 2 breaths.

- Make sure the child is lying faceup on a firm, flat surface.
- Quickly move bulky clothes out of the way. If a child's clothes are difficult to remove, you can still provide compressions over clothing.
  - If an AED becomes available, remove all clothes that cover the chest. AED pads must not be placed over any clothing.
- Give 30 chest compressions.
  - Use either 1 or 2 hands to give compressions.
    - **1 hand:** Put the heel of one hand on the center of the chest (over the lower half of the breastbone).
    - **2 hands:** Put the heel of one hand on the center of the chest (over the lower half of the breastbone). Put your other hand on top of the first hand.
  - Push straight down at least one third the depth of the chest, or approximately 2 inches.
  - Push at a rate of 100 to 120/min. Count the compressions out loud.
  - Let the chest come back up to its normal position after each compression.
- After 30 compressions, give 2 breaths.
  - Open the airway and give 2 breaths (blow for 1 second for each). Watch for the chest to begin to rise as you give each breath.
- Try not to interrupt compressions for more than 10 seconds, even when you give breaths.

Use an AED

CPR combined with using an AED provides the best chance of saving a life. If possible, use an AED every time you provide CPR. AEDs can be used for children and infants as well as for adults.

Some AEDs can deliver a smaller shock dose for children and infants if you use child pads or a child-cable key or switch.

- If the AED can deliver the smaller shock dose, use it for infants and children less than 8 years of age.
- If the AED cannot deliver a child shock dose, you can use the adult pads and give an adult shock dose for infants and children less than 8 years of age.

AEDs are safe, accurate, and easy to use. Once you turn on the AED, follow the prompts. The AED will check to see if the child needs a shock and will automatically give one or tell you when to give one.

Turn on the AED

To use an AED, turn it on by either pushing the On button or lifting the lid (Figure 42). Once you turn on the AED, you will hear prompts that tell you everything you need to do.

Figure 42. Turning on the AED.

Attach the Pads

Many AEDs have pads for adults and a child pad–cable system or key for children and infants.

- Use child pads if the child or infant is younger than 8 years. If child pads are not available, use adult pads.
- Use adult pads if the child is 8 years or older.

Before you place the pads, quickly scan the child to see if there are any special situations that might require additional steps (see Special Situations later in this section).

Peel away the backing from the pads. Follow the pictures on the pads, and attach them to the child's bare chest (Figure 43).

When you put the pads on the chest, make sure they don't touch each other. If the child's chest is small, the pads may overlap. In this case, you may need to put one pad on the child's chest and the other on the child's back. Plug the pads connector into the AED, if necessary.

Figure 43. Place pads on a child by following the pictures on the pads.

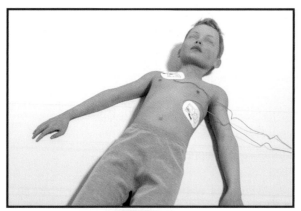

Clear the Child if a Shock Is Advised

Let the AED analyze the heart rhythm. If the AED advises a shock, it will tell you to stay clear of the child. If so, then loudly state, "Clear." Make sure that no one is touching the child just before you push the Shock button (Figure 44).

Figure 44. Make sure that no one is touching the child just before you push the Shock button.

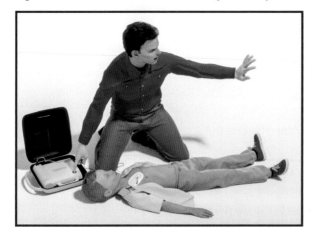

Steps for Using an AED for a Child

Use the AED as soon as it's available. Here are the steps for using the AED for a child:

- Turn the AED on and follow the prompts.
  - Turn it on by pushing the On button or lifting the lid.
  - Follow the prompts, which will tell you everything you need to do.
- Attach the pads.
  - Use child pads if the child is less than 8 years of age. If child pads are not available, use adult pads.
  - Use adult pads if the child is 8 years or older.
  - Peel away the backing from the pads.
  - Following the pictures on the pads, attach them to the child's bare chest. Make sure the pads don't touch each other. If the pads will touch, put one pad on the child's chest and the other on the child's back.
  - Plug the pads connector into the AED, if necessary.
- Let the AED analyze.
  - Loudly state, "Clear," and make sure that no one is touching the child.
  - The AED will analyze the heart rhythm.
  - If the AED tells you that a shock is not needed, resume CPR.
- Deliver a shock if needed.
  - Loudly state, "Clear," and make sure that no one is touching the child.
  - Push the Shock button.
  - Immediately resume CPR.

Special Situations

Some special situations can affect how you place the AED pads. Although it is not very common, you may encounter a medicine patch or a device on a child, which may interfere with the AED pad placement. So before you apply the pads, quickly scan the child and assess the situation to check for the following:

- *If the child is lying in water*
  - Quickly move the child to a dry area.
- *If the child is lying on snow or in a small puddle*
  - You can use the AED (the chest doesn't have to be completely dry).
  - If the chest is covered with water or sweat, quickly wipe it before attaching the pads.
- *If there is water on the child's chest*
  - Quickly wipe the chest dry before attaching the pads.
- *If the child has an implanted defibrillator or pacemaker*
  - Don't put the AED pad directly over the implanted device.
  - Follow the normal steps for operating an AED.
- *If there is a medicine patch where you need to place an AED pad*
  - Don't put the AED pad directly over a medicine patch.
  - Use protective gloves.
  - Remove the medicated patch.
  - Wipe the area clean.
  - Attach the AED pads.
- *If the child is wearing jewelry*
  - You don't need to remove a child's jewelry as long as it doesn't interfere with the placement of the pads or touch the pads. It does not cause a shock hazard to either the child or rescuer.

Continue Providing CPR and Using the AED

As soon as the AED gives the shock, immediately resume chest compressions. Continue to follow the AED prompts as they guide you.

Provide CPR and use the AED until

- Someone else arrives who can take turns providing CPR with you
  - If someone else arrives, you can take turns giving compressions. Switch rescuers about every 2 minutes, which is about 5 cycles of compressions or breaths, or sooner if you get tired.
- The child begins to move, speak, blink, or otherwise react
- Someone with more advanced training arrives

Putting It All Together: Child High-Quality CPR AED Summary

Children usually have healthy hearts. Often, a child's heart stops because the child can't breathe or is having trouble breathing. For this reason, it's very important to give breaths as well as compressions to a child.

Compressions are still very important to deliver blood flow. They are the core of CPR. Try not to interrupt chest compressions for more than 10 seconds when you give breaths.

Assess and Get Help
- Make sure the scene is safe.
- Tap and shout (check for responsiveness).
  - If the child is responsive, ask, "Do you need help?"
  - If the child is unresponsive, go to the next step.
- Shout for help.
- Check for breathing.
  - If the child is breathing, stay with the child until advanced help arrives.
  - If the child is not breathing or only gasping, begin CPR and use the AED. See the next steps.

Phone 9-1-1, Begin CPR, and Get an AED

If someone comes to help and a cell phone is available

- Ask the person to phone 9-1-1 on the cell phone, put it on speaker mode, and go get an AED while you begin CPR.
- Use the AED as soon as it is available.

If someone comes to help and a cell phone is not available

- Ask the person to go phone 9-1-1 and get an AED while you begin CPR.
- Use the AED as soon as it is available.

If you are alone and have a cell phone or nearby phone

- Phone 9-1-1 and put the phone on speaker mode while you begin CPR.
- Give 5 sets of 30 compressions and 2 breaths.
- Go get an AED, and use it as soon as it is available.
- Return to the child and continue CPR.

If you are alone and don't have a cell phone

- Give 5 sets of 30 compressions and 2 breaths.
- Go phone 9-1-1 and get an AED; use the AED as soon as it is available.
- Return to the child and continue CPR.

Provide High-Quality CPR

When providing CPR, give sets of 30 compressions and 2 breaths.

- Make sure the child is lying faceup on a firm, flat surface.
- Quickly move bulky clothes out of the way. If a child's clothes are difficult to remove, you can still provide compressions over clothing.
  - If an AED becomes available, remove all clothes that cover the chest. AED pads must not be placed over any clothing.
- Give 30 chest compressions.
  - Use 1 or 2 hands to give compressions.
    - **1 hand:** Put the heel of one hand on the center of the chest (over the lower half of the breastbone).
    - **2 hands:** Put the heel of one hand on the center of the chest (over the lower half of the breastbone). Put your other hand on top of the first hand.
  - Push straight down at least one third the depth of the chest, or approximately 2 inches.
  - Push at a rate of 100 to 120/min. Count the compressions out loud.
  - Let the chest come back up to its normal position after each compression.
- After 30 compressions, give 2 breaths.
  - Open the airway and give 2 breaths (blow for 1 second for each). Watch for the chest to begin to rise as you give each breath.
  - Try not to interrupt compressions for more than 10 seconds, even when you give breaths.
- Use an AED as soon as it is available.
  - Turn the AED on and follow the prompts.
  - Attach the pads.
    - Use child pads if the child is less than 8 years of age. If child pads are not available, use adult pads.
    - Use adult pads if the child is 8 years or older.
  - Let the AED analyze.
  - Make sure that no one is touching the child, and deliver a shock if advised.
- Provide CPR and use the AED until
  - Someone else arrives who can take turns providing CPR with you
  - The child begins to move, speak, blink, or otherwise react
  - Someone with more advanced training arrives and takes over

CPR for Infants

In this section, you will learn when CPR is needed and how to give CPR to an infant.

Definition of an Infant

For the purposes of this course, an infant is less than 1 year old.

Differences in CPR for Infants vs CPR for Children and Adults

Because infants are so small, there are some differences in how you perform CPR for them compared with what you do for children or adults. When giving chest compressions to an infant, you use only 2 fingers of 1 hand or 2 thumbs—vs 1 or 2 hands for a child and 2 hands for an adult.

For an infant, you should push down about 1½ inches at the rate of 100 to 120/min.

Topics covered in this section are

- Assessing and phoning 9-1-1
- Performing high-quality CPR
- Putting it all together: infant high-quality CPR summary

Assess and Phone 9-1-1

When you see an infant who may have had a cardiac arrest, take the following 5 steps to assess the emergency and get help:

1. Make sure the scene is safe.
2. Tap and shout (check for responsiveness).
3. Shout for help.
4. Check for breathing.
5. Phone 9-1-1, begin CPR, and get an AED.

Depending on the circumstance and resources you have available, you may be able to perform some of these actions at the same time. You might, for example, phone 9-1-1 with your cell phone on speaker mode while checking for breathing.

Step 1: Make Sure the Scene Is Safe

Before you assess the infant, look for anything nearby that might hurt you. You can't help if you get hurt too.

As you help, be aware if anything changes and makes it unsafe for you or the infant.

Step 2: Tap and Shout (Check for Responsiveness)

Tap and shout to check if the infant is responsive or unresponsive (Figure 45). Tap the infant's foot and shout their name.

- If they move, cry, blink, or otherwise react when you tap their foot, they're responsive; continue first aid care.
- If they don't move, cry, blink, or otherwise react when you tap their foot, they're unresponsive. Shout for help so that if others are nearby, they can help you.

Figure 45. Tap and shout (check for responsiveness).

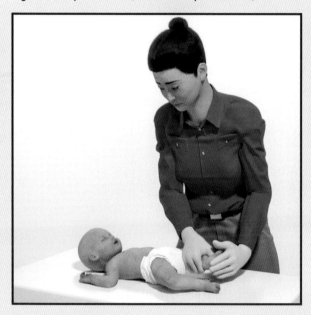

Step 3: Shout for Help

In an emergency, the sooner you realize that there's a problem and get help, the better it is for the infant with a cardiac arrest. When more people are helping, you can provide better care to the infant.

If the infant is unresponsive, shout for help (Figure 46). If someone comes, send that person to phone 9-1-1 and get an AED. If you have a cell phone, phone 9-1-1 and put it on speaker mode.

Figure 46. Shout for help.

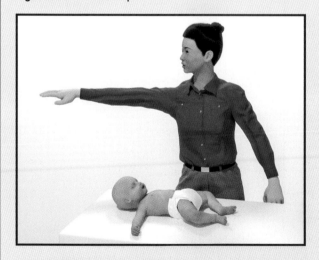

Step 4: Check for Breathing

If the infant is unresponsive, check for breathing (Figure 47).

Scan the chest repeatedly for at least 5 seconds (but no more than 10 seconds), looking for the chest to rise and fall. If the infant is not breathing or is only gasping, they need CPR.

If the infant is unresponsive and is breathing

- This infant does not need CPR.
- Roll them onto their side (if you don't suspect a neck or back injury). This will help keep the airway clear in case the infant vomits.
- If no one has done so, phone 9-1-1, and then return to the infant.
- If the infant is having breathing problems, help them. See Breathing Problems (Asthma) in Part 2.
- Stay with the infant until advanced help arrives.

If the infant is unresponsive and not breathing or is only gasping

- This infant needs CPR.
- Make sure the infant is lying faceup on a firm, flat surface.
- Have someone phone 9-1-1, or use your cell phone (or nearby phone), put it on speaker mode, and phone 9-1-1.
- Begin CPR. Give 5 sets of 30 compressions and 2 breaths.
- After 5 sets of compressions and breaths, phone 9-1-1 and get an AED (if no one has done this yet). Use the AED as soon as it is available.

Remember: Unresponsive + No breathing or only gasping = Provide CPR

Figure 47. Check for breathing.

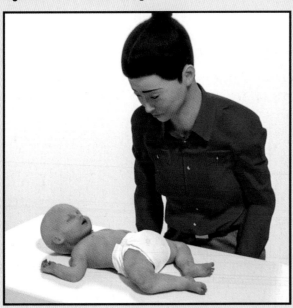

Step 5: Phone 9-1-1, Begin CPR, and Get an AED

If someone comes to help and a cell phone is available

- Ask the person to phone 9-1-1 on the cell phone, put it on speaker mode, and go get an AED while you begin CPR.
- Use the AED as soon as it is available.

If someone comes to help and a cell phone is not available

- Ask the person to go phone 9-1-1 and get an AED while you begin CPR.
- Use the AED as soon as it is available.

If you are alone and have a cell phone or a nearby phone

- Phone 9-1-1 and put the phone on speaker mode while you begin CPR.
- Give 5 sets of 30 compressions and 2 breaths.
- Go get an AED. If the infant isn't injured and you're alone, you can carry the infant with you while you go to phone 9-1-1 and get an AED (Figure 48). Use the AED as soon as it is available.
- Return to the infant and continue CPR.

If you are alone and don't have a cell phone

- Give 5 sets of 30 compressions and 2 breaths.
- Go phone 9-1-1 and get an AED. If the infant isn't injured and you're alone, you can carry the infant with you while you go to phone 9-1-1 and get an AED. Use the AED as soon as it is available.
- Return to the infant and continue CPR.

Figure 48. Take the infant with you while you go to phone 9-1-1 and get an AED.

Follow the Dispatcher's Instructions

Stay on the phone until the 9-1-1 dispatcher tells you to hang up. Answering the dispatcher's questions will not delay the arrival of help.

The dispatcher will ask you about the emergency—where you are and what has happened. Dispatchers can provide instructions that will help you, such as telling you how to provide CPR, use an AED, or give first aid.

That's why it's important to put the phone on speaker mode after phoning 9-1-1. It allows the dispatcher and the person providing CPR to speak to each other.

What to Do if You Are Not Sure

It's better to give CPR to an infant who doesn't need it than not to give it to an infant who does need it. CPR is not likely to cause harm if the infant is not in cardiac arrest. But without CPR, an infant who is in cardiac arrest may die.

So if you aren't sure, provide CPR. You may save an infant's life.

Summary

Here is a summary of how to assess the emergency and get help when you encounter an ill or injured infant:

Assess and Get Help

- Make sure the scene is safe.
- Tap and shout (check for responsiveness).
  - If the infant is responsive, continue first aid care.
  - If the infant is unresponsive, go to the next step. Shout for help.
- Check for breathing.
  - If the infant is unresponsive but breathing, they don't need CPR.
    - Roll them onto their side (if you don't think they have a neck or back injury).
    - If no one has done so, phone 9-1-1.
    - Stay with the infant until advanced help arrives.
    - If the infant is unresponsive and not breathing or is only gasping, begin CPR and use an AED. See the next steps.

Phone 9-1-1, Begin CPR, and Get an AED

- *If someone comes to help and a cell phone is available*
  - Ask the person to phone 9-1-1 and get an AED. Ask them to put the phone on speaker mode so that you can hear the dispatcher's instructions.
  - Check the infant's breathing, and begin CPR if needed.
- *If you are alone and have a cell phone or a nearby phone*
  - Phone 9-1-1 and put the phone on speaker mode while you begin CPR.
  - Give 5 sets of 30 compressions and 2 breaths.
  - Go get an AED. If the infant isn't injured and you're alone, take the infant with you while you go to phone 9-1-1 and get an AED. Use the AED as soon as it's available.
  - Return to the infant and continue CPR.
  - Resume CPR and using the AED until advanced help arrives and takes over.
- *If you are alone and don't have a cell phone*
  - Check the infant's breathing, and begin CPR if needed.
  - Give 5 sets of 30 compressions and 2 breaths.
  - Go phone 9-1-1, and get an AED. Return to the infant. If the infant isn't injured and you're alone, after 5 sets of 30 compressions and 2 breaths, you can carry the infant with you while you go to phone 9-1-1 and get an AED.
  - Resume CPR and using the AED until advanced help arrives and takes over.
- Continue providing CPR and using the AED until
  - Someone else arrives who can take turns providing CPR with you
  - The infant begins to move, speak, cry, blink, or otherwise react
  - Someone with more advanced training arrives

Perform High-Quality CPR

Learning how to perform high-quality CPR is important. The better you can perform CPR skills, the better the chances of survival, whether you are helping an adult, a child, or an infant.

CPR has 2 main skills: providing compressions and giving breaths. In this section, you will learn how to perform these skills for an infant in cardiac arrest.

Provide Compressions

You already learned that compressions are the most important part of CPR because they help pump blood to the brain and other organs. Pushing hard and fast when giving compressions is just as important for infants as it is for children and adults.

To perform high-quality CPR, make sure that you

- Provide compressions that are deep enough
- Provide compressions that are fast enough
- Let the chest come back up to its normal position after each compression
- Try not to interrupt compressions for more than 10 seconds, even when you give breaths

Compression depth is an important part of providing high-quality compressions. You need to push hard enough to pump blood through the body. It's better to push too hard than not hard enough. People are often afraid of injuring an infant by providing compressions, but injury is unlikely.

Compression Techniques

One of the main differences in infant CPR is that you can use just 2 fingers or 2 thumbs to provide compressions. You can also use the heel of 1 hand if you aren't able to push deep enough. See Figure 49 for the correct placement of your fingers and thumbs on the infant's breastbone, just below the nipple line. Push straight down at least one third the depth of the chest, or approximately 1½ inches.

Here is how to provide compressions for an infant during CPR:

- Make sure the infant is lying faceup on a firm, flat surface.
- Quickly move bulky clothes out of the way. If an infant's clothes are difficult to remove, you can still provide compressions over clothing.
  - If an AED becomes available, remove all clothes that cover the chest. AED pads must not be placed over any clothing.
- Use 2 fingers, 2 thumbs, or 1 hand to give compressions.
  - **2 fingers:** Place your fingers on the breastbone, just below the nipple line (Figure 49A).
  - **2 thumbs:** Place both thumbs side by side on the breastbone, just below the nipple line. Encircle the infant's chest and support the infant's back with the fingers of both hands (Figure 49B).
  - **1 hand:** Use the heel of 1 hand to give compressions. Place your hand on the breastbone, just below the nipple line.
- Push straight down at least one third the depth of the chest, or about 1½ inches.
- Push at a rate of 100 to 120/min. Count the compressions out loud.
- Let the chest come back up to its normal position after each compression.

Figure 49. Infant compressions. **A,** Use 2 fingers of 1 hand to give compressions. **B,** Use 2 thumbs to give compressions. Place them on the breastbone, just below the nipple line. Avoid the tip of the breastbone.

A

B

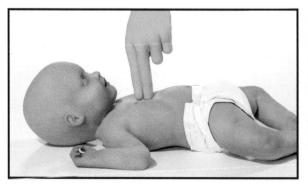
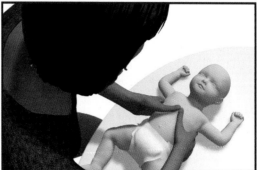

Switch Rescuers to Avoid Fatigue

Performing chest compressions correctly is hard work. The more tired you become, the less effective your compressions will be.

If someone else knows CPR, you can take turns giving compressions. Switch rescuers about every 2 minutes, or sooner if you get tired. Move quickly to keep any pauses in compressions as short as possible.

Remind other rescuers to perform high-quality CPR as described in this workbook.

Give Breaths

The second skill of CPR is giving breaths. After each set of 30 compressions, you will need to give 2 breaths.

Infants often have healthy hearts, but even an infant's heart can stop beating if they can't breathe or have trouble breathing. So it's very important to give breaths as well as compressions to an infant who needs CPR.

When you give breaths, look at the infant's chest to see if it begins to rise. For infants, you will not need to blow as much as for larger children. When you can see the chest rise, you know you have delivered an effective breath.

Open the Airway

Before giving breaths, open the airway. This lifts the tongue from the back of the throat to make sure your breaths get air into the lungs.

Opening the infant's airway too far can actually close the infant's airway, making it difficult to get air inside. Follow these steps to make sure you open the infant's airway correctly:

- Put one hand on the forehead and the fingers of your other hand on the bony part of the chin. Avoid pressing into the soft part of the neck or under the chin because this might block the airway. Also, don't push the head back too far. This might close the airway.
- Tilt the head back and lift the chin.

Pocket Masks for Giving Breaths

You may give breaths with or without a barrier device, such as a pocket mask. These plastic devices fit over the infant's mouth and nose. They protect the rescuer from blood, vomit, or disease. Your instructor may discuss other types of barrier devices, like face shields, that you can use when giving breaths.

There are different kinds of pocket masks as well as different sizes. So make sure you use the right size for an infant. Pocket masks are typically made of hard plastic with a 1-way valve, which is the part you breathe into. You may need to put a pocket mask together before using it.

Give Breaths Without a Pocket Mask

Giving someone breaths without a barrier device is usually quite safe. Use your best judgment on whether it's safe for you to give breaths without a barrier device.

Follow these steps to give breaths without a pocket mask or face shield:

- While holding the airway open, take a normal breath. Cover the infant's mouth and nose with your mouth (Figure 50). If you have difficulty making an effective seal, try either a mouth-to-mouth or a mouth-to-nose breath.
  - If you use the mouth-to-mouth technique, pinch the nose closed.
  - If you use the mouth-to-nose technique, close the mouth.
- Give 2 breaths (blow for 1 second for each). Watch for the chest to begin to rise as you give each breath.
- Try not to interrupt compressions for more than 10 seconds, even when you give breaths.

Figure 50. Cover the infant's mouth and nose with your mouth.

Give Breaths With a Pocket Mask

Follow these steps to give breaths with a pocket mask:

- Put the mask over the infant's mouth and nose.
  - If the mask has a pointed end, put the narrow end of the mask on the bridge of the nose; position the wide end so it covers the mouth.
- Tilt the head and lift the chin while pressing the mask against the infant's face. It's important to make an airtight seal between the infant's face and the mask while you lift the chin to keep the airway open (Figure 51).
- Give 2 breaths (blow for 1 second for each). Watch for the chest to begin to rise as you give each breath.
- Try not to interrupt compressions for more than 10 seconds, even when you give breaths.

Figure 51. Giving breaths with a pocket mask.

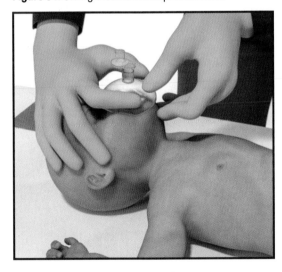

What to Do if the Chest Doesn't Rise

It takes a little practice to give breaths correctly. If you give someone a breath and the chest doesn't rise, do the following:

- Allow the head to go back to its normal position.
- Open the airway again by tilting the head back and lifting the chin.
- Then, give another breath. Make sure the chest rises.

Minimize Interruptions in Chest Compressions

If you have been unable to give 2 effective breaths in 10 seconds, go back to pushing hard and fast on the chest. Try to give breaths again after every 30 compressions.

Don't interrupt compressions for more than 10 seconds.

Give Sets of 30 Compressions and 2 Breaths

When providing CPR, give sets of 30 compressions and 2 breaths.

- Make sure the infant is lying faceup on a firm, flat surface.
- Quickly move bulky clothes out of the way. If an infant's clothes are difficult to remove, you can still provide compressions over clothing.
  - If an AED becomes available, remove all clothes that cover the chest. AED pads must not be placed over any clothing.
- Give 30 chest compressions.
  - Use 2 fingers of 1 hand or 2 thumbs to give compressions. Place them on the breastbone, just below the nipple line.
  - Push straight down at least one third the depth of the chest or approximately 1½ inches. If you can't push down this far, you can use the heel of 1 hand to give compressions.

- Push at a rate of 100 to 120/min. Count the compressions out loud.
  - Let the chest come back up to its normal position after each compression.
- After 30 compressions, give 2 breaths.
  - Open the airway and give 2 breaths (blow for 1 second for each). Watch for the chest to begin to rise as you give each breath.
- Try not to interrupt compressions for more than 10 seconds, even when you give breaths.

Do Not Delay CPR to Get an AED for an Infant

CPR with both compressions and breaths is the most important thing you can do for an infant in cardiac arrest. Do not delay CPR to get an AED for an infant. If someone brings an AED to you, use it as soon as it arrives (see the Use an AED section in CPR and AED Use for Children).

Putting It All Together: Infant High-Quality CPR Summary

Infants usually have healthy hearts. Often, an infant's heart stops because the infant can't breathe or is having trouble breathing. As a result, it's very important to give breaths as well as compressions to an infant.

Compressions are still very important to deliver blood flow and are the core of CPR. Try not to interrupt chest compressions for more than 10 seconds when you give breaths.

Assess and Get Help
- Make sure the scene is safe.
- Tap and shout (check for responsiveness).
  - If the infant is responsive, continue first aid care.
  - If the infant is unresponsive, go to the next step.
- Shout for help.
- Check for breathing.
  - If the infant is breathing, stay with the infant until advanced help arrives.
  - If the infant is not breathing or is only gasping, begin CPR and use the AED. See the next steps.

Phone 9-1-1, Begin CPR, and Get an AED

If someone comes to help and a cell phone is available

- Ask the person to phone 9-1-1 on the cell phone, put it on speaker mode, and go get an AED while you begin CPR.
- Use the AED as soon as it is available.

If someone comes to help and a cell phone is not available

- Ask the person to go phone 9-1-1 and get an AED while you begin CPR.
- Use the AED as soon as it is available.

If you are alone and have a cell phone or nearby phone

- Phone 9-1-1 and put the phone on speaker mode while you begin CPR.
- Give 5 sets of 30 compressions and 2 breaths.
- Go get an AED. If the infant isn't injured and you're alone, you can carry the infant with you while you go to phone 9-1-1 and get an AED. Use the AED as soon as it is available.
- Return to the infant and continue CPR.

If you are alone and don't have a cell phone

- Give 5 sets of 30 compressions and 2 breaths.
- Go phone 9-1-1 and get an AED. If the infant isn't injured and you're alone, after 5 sets of 30 compressions and 2 breaths, you can carry the infant with you while you go to phone 9-1-1 and get an AED. Use the AED as soon as it is available.
- Return to the infant and continue CPR.

Provide High-Quality CPR

When providing CPR, give sets of 30 compressions and 2 breaths.

- Make sure the infant is lying faceup on a firm, flat surface.
- Quickly move bulky clothes out of the way. If an infant's clothes are difficult to remove, you can still provide compressions over clothing.
  - If an AED becomes available, remove all clothes that cover the chest. AED pads must not be placed over any clothing.
- Give 30 chest compressions.
  - Use 2 fingers of 1 hand or 2 thumbs to give compressions. Place them on the breastbone, just below the nipple line.
  - Push straight down at least one third the depth of the chest, or about 1½ inches. If you are unable to push down this far, you can use the heel of 1 hand to give compressions.
  - Push at a rate of 100 to 120/min. Count the compressions out loud.
  - Let the chest come back up to its normal position after each compression.
- After 30 compressions, give 2 breaths.
  - Open the airway and give 2 breaths (blow for 1 second for each). Watch for the chest to begin to rise as you give each breath.
  - Try not to interrupt compressions for more than 10 seconds, even when you give breaths.
- Use an AED as soon as it is available.
  - Turn the AED on and follow the prompts.
  - Attach the pads.
    - Use child pads for an infant if available.
    - If child pads are not available, use adult pads.
  - Let the AED analyze.
  - Make sure that no one is touching the infant, and deliver a shock if advised.
- Provide CPR and use the AED until
  - Someone else arrives who can take turns providing CPR with you
  - The infant begins to move, cry, blink, or otherwise react
  - Someone with more advanced training arrives and takes over

CPR and AED Use for Adults

In this section, you'll learn when CPR is needed, how to give CPR to an adult, and how to use an AED.

Adult Chain of Survival

The AHA adult Chain of Survival (Figure 52) shows the most important actions needed to treat adults who have cardiac arrests outside of a hospital. In this section, you'll learn about the first 3 links of the chain. The fourth and fifth links are advanced care provided by emergency responders and hospital providers who will take over care, and the sixth link is recovery.

Remember that seconds count when someone has a cardiac arrest. Wherever you are, take action. The adult Chain of Survival starts with you!

- **First link:** Immediately recognize the emergency and phone 9-1-1.
- **Second link:** Perform early CPR with an emphasis on chest compressions.
- **Third link:** Use an AED immediately (as soon as it is available).
- **Fourth and fifth links:** Advanced care is provided.
- **Sixth link:** Additional treatment, observation, and rehabilitation may be needed to fully recover from a cardiac arrest.

Figure 52. The AHA adult Chain of Survival for cardiac arrests that happen outside of a hospital.

Topics covered in this section are
- Assessing and phoning 9-1-1
- Performing high-quality CPR
- Using an AED
- Putting it all together: adult high-quality CPR AED summary

Assess and Phone 9-1-1

When you see an adult who may have had a cardiac arrest, take the following 5 steps to assess the emergency and get help:

1. Make sure the scene is safe.
2. Tap and shout (check for responsiveness).
3. Shout for help.
4. Phone 9-1-1 and get an AED.
5. Check for breathing.

Depending on the particular circumstance and the resources you have available, you may be able to perform some of these actions at the same time. You might, for example, phone 9-1-1 with your cell phone on speaker mode while you are checking for breathing.

Step 1: Make Sure the Scene Is Safe

Before you begin to help the person, look for anything nearby that might hurt you. You can't help if you get hurt too.

As you help, be aware if anything changes and makes it unsafe for you or the person needing help.

Step 2: Tap and Shout (Check for Responsiveness)

Tap and shout to check whether the person is responsive or unresponsive (Figure 53). Lean over the person or kneel at their side. Tap their shoulders and ask if they're OK.

- If they move, speak, blink, or otherwise react when you tap their shoulders, they're responsive. Ask if they need help.
- If they don't move, speak, blink, or otherwise react when you tap their shoulders, they're unresponsive. Shout for help so that if others are nearby, they can help you.

Figure 53. Tap and shout (check for responsiveness).

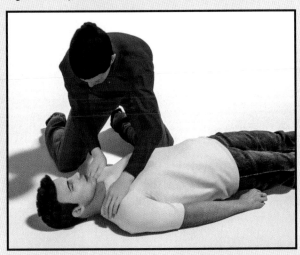

Step 3: Shout for Help

In an emergency, the sooner you realize that there's a problem and get additional help, the better it is for the person with a cardiac arrest. When more people are helping, you can provide better care to the person.

If the person you are helping is unresponsive, shout for help (Figure 54).

Figure 54. Shout for help.

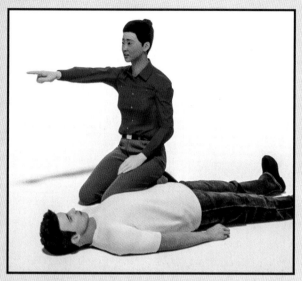

Step 4: Phone 9-1-1 and Get an AED

If someone comes to help and a cell phone is available

- Ask the person to phone 9-1-1 and get an AED. Say, "You—phone 9-1-1 and get an AED."
- Ask them to put the phone on speaker mode so that you can hear the dispatcher's instructions.

If someone comes to help and a cell phone is not available

- Ask the person to go phone 9-1-1 and get an AED while you continue providing emergency care.

If you are alone and have a cell phone or nearby phone

- If no one comes to help, phone 9-1-1. Put the phone on speaker mode so that you can hear the dispatcher's instructions while you continue providing emergency care.
- If an AED is needed, you will have to go get it yourself.

If you are alone and don't have a cell phone

- Leave the person to go phone 9-1-1 and get an AED.
- Return and continue providing emergency care.

Follow the Dispatcher's Instructions

Stay on the phone until the 9-1-1 dispatcher tells you to hang up. Answering the dispatcher's questions will not delay the arrival of help.

The dispatcher will ask you about the emergency—where you are and what has happened. Dispatchers can provide instructions that will help you, such as telling you how to provide CPR, use an AED, or give first aid.

That's why it's important to put the phone on speaker mode after phoning 9-1-1. It allows the dispatcher and the person providing CPR to speak to each other.

Step 5: Check for Breathing

If the person is unresponsive, check for breathing (Figure 55).

Scan the person from head to chest repeatedly for at least 5 seconds (but no more than 10 seconds), looking for chest rise and fall. If the person is not breathing or is only gasping, they need CPR.

If the person is unresponsive and is breathing

- This person does not need CPR.
- Roll them onto their side (if you don't think they have a neck or back injury). This will help keep the airway clear in case they vomit.
- Stay with the person until advanced help arrives.

If the person is unresponsive and not breathing or is only gasping

- This person needs CPR.
- Make sure the person is lying faceup on a firm, flat surface.
- Begin CPR.

Remember: Unresponsive + No breathing or only gasping = Provide CPR

Figure 55. Check for breathing.

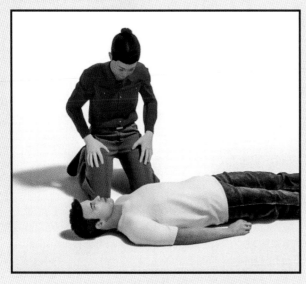

What to Do if You Are Not Sure

It's better to give CPR to someone who doesn't need it than not to give it to someone who does need it. CPR is not likely to harm someone who is not in cardiac arrest. But without CPR, someone who is in cardiac arrest may die.

So if you aren't sure, provide CPR. You may save a life.

Summary

Here is a summary of how to assess the emergency and get help when you encounter an ill or injured adult:

Assess and Phone 9-1-1

- Make sure the scene is safe.
- Tap and shout (check for responsiveness).
  - If the person is responsive, ask if they need help.
  - If the person is unresponsive, go to the next step.
- Shout for help.
- Phone 9-1-1 and get an AED.
  - Phone or send someone to phone 9-1-1 and get an AED.
  - If you're alone and have a cell phone or a nearby phone, put it on speaker mode and phone 9-1-1.
  - If you're alone and don't have a nearby phone, leave the person while you go phone 9-1-1 and get an AED.
- Check for breathing.
  - If the person is breathing normally, stay with the person until advanced help arrives.
  - If the person is not breathing normally or is only gasping, begin CPR and use an AED.

Perform High-Quality CPR

Learning how to perform high-quality CPR is important. The better you can perform the CPR skills, the better the person's chances of survival, whether you are helping an adult, a child, or an infant.

CPR has 2 main skills: providing compressions and giving breaths. You will learn how to perform these skills for an adult in cardiac arrest in this section.

Provide Compressions

To provide high-quality compressions, make sure that you

- Provide compressions that are deep enough
- Provide compressions that are fast enough
- Let the chest come back up to its normal position after each compression
- Try not to interrupt compressions for more than 10 seconds, even when you give breaths

Compression depth is an important part of providing high-quality compressions. You need to push hard enough to pump blood through the body. It's better to push too hard than not hard enough. People are often afraid of injuring someone by providing compressions, but injury is unlikely.

Compression Technique

Here is how to provide compressions for an adult during CPR:

- Make sure the person is lying faceup on a firm, flat surface.
- Quickly move bulky clothes out of the way. If their clothes are difficult to remove, you can still provide compressions over clothing.
  - If an AED becomes available, remove all clothes that cover the chest. AED pads must not be placed over any clothing.
- Put the heel of one hand on the center of the chest, over the lower half of the breastbone. Put your other hand on top of the first hand (Figure 56).
- Push straight down at least 2 inches, or 5 cm.
- Push at a rate of 100 to 120/min. Count the compressions out loud.
- Let the chest come back up to its normal position after each compression.
- Try not to interrupt compressions for more than 10 seconds, even when you give breaths.

Compressions for a Pregnant Woman

- Do not delay providing chest compressions for a pregnant woman in cardiac arrest. High-quality CPR can increase the mother's and the infant's chance of survival. If you do not perform CPR on a pregnant woman when needed, the lives of both the mother and the infant are at risk.
- Perform high-quality chest compressions for a pregnant woman in cardiac arrest as you would for any victim of cardiac arrest. If the woman begins to move, speak, blink or otherwise react, stop CPR and roll her onto her left side.

Figure 56. Compressions. **A,** Put the heel of one hand on the center of the chest (lower half of the breastbone). **B,** Put the other hand on top of the first hand.

A

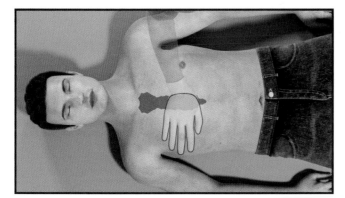

B

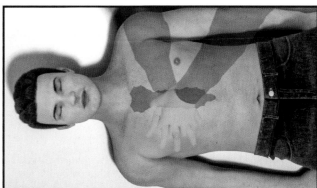

Switch Rescuers to Avoid Fatigue

Performing chest compressions correctly is hard work. The more tired you become, the less effective your compressions will be.

If someone else knows CPR, you can take turns providing CPR (Figure 57). Switch rescuers about every 2 minutes, or sooner if you get tired. Move quickly to keep any pauses in compressions as short as possible.

Remind other rescuers to perform high-quality CPR as described in this workbook.

Figure 57. Switch rescuers about every 2 minutes to avoid fatigue.

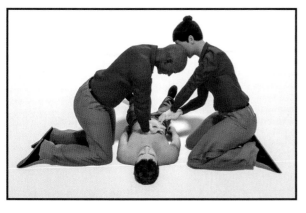

Give Breaths

The second skill of CPR is giving breaths. After each set of 30 compressions, you will need to give 2 breaths. You may give breaths with or without a barrier device, such as a pocket mask or face shield.

When you give breaths, the breaths need to make the chest rise visibly. When you can see the chest rise, you know you have delivered an effective breath.

Open the Airway

Before giving breaths, open the airway (Figure 58). This lifts the tongue from the back of the throat to make sure your breaths get air into the lungs.

Follow these steps to open the airway:

- Put one hand on the forehead and the fingers of your other hand on the bony part of the chin. Avoid pressing into the soft part of the neck or under the chin because this might block the airway.
- Tilt the head back and lift the chin.

Figure 58. Open the airway by tilting the head back and lifting the chin.

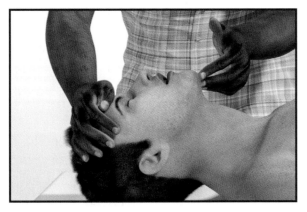

Give Breaths Without a Pocket Mask

Giving someone breaths without a barrier device is usually quite safe. Use your best judgment on whether it's safe for you to give breaths without a barrier device.

- While holding the airway open, pinch the nose closed with your thumb and forefinger.
- Take a normal breath. Cover the person's mouth with your mouth.
- Give 2 breaths (blow for 1 second for each). Watch for the chest to begin to rise as you give each breath (Figure 59).

- Try not to interrupt compressions for more than 10 seconds, even when you give breaths.

Figure 59. Giving breaths without a barrier device .

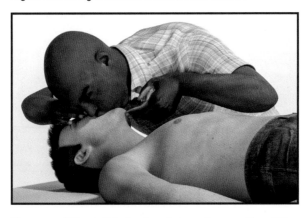

Pocket Masks for Giving Breaths

Pocket masks are made of hard plastic and fit over the person's mouth and nose (Figure 60). They protect the rescuer from blood, vomit, or disease. Your instructor may discuss other types of barrier devices, like face shields, that can be used when giving breaths.

If you're in the workplace, your employer may provide PPE, including pocket masks or face shields, for use during CPR.

There are different kinds of pocket masks as well as different sizes for adults, children, and infants. So make sure you're using the right size. Pocket masks typically include a 1-way valve, which is the part you breathe into. You may need to put the pocket mask and valve together before you use it.

Figure 60. Some people use a pocket mask when giving breaths.

Give Breaths With a Pocket Mask

Follow these steps to give breaths with a pocket mask (Figure 61):

- Put the mask over the person's mouth and nose.
  - If the mask has a narrow, pointed end, put that end of the mask on the bridge of the nose; position the wide end so that it covers the mouth.
- Tilt the head and lift the chin while pressing the mask against the person's face. It's important to make an airtight seal between the person's face and the mask while you lift the chin to keep the airway open.
- Give 2 breaths (blow for 1 second for each). Watch for the chest to begin to rise as you give each breath.
- Try not to interrupt compressions for more than 10 seconds, even when you give breaths.

Figure 61. Giving breaths with a pocket mask.

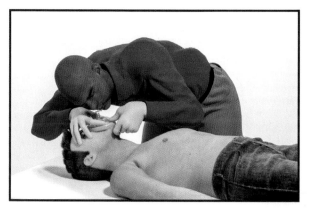

What to Do if the Chest Doesn't Rise

It takes a little practice to give breaths correctly. If you give someone a breath and the chest doesn't rise, do the following:

- Allow the head to go back to its normal position.
- Open the airway again by tilting the head back and lifting the chin.
- Then, give another breath. Make sure the chest rises.

Minimize Interruptions in Chest Compressions

If you have been unable to give 2 effective breaths in 10 seconds, go back to pushing hard and fast on the chest. Try to give breaths again after every 30 compressions. Don't interrupt compressions for more than 10 seconds.

Give Sets of 30 Compressions and 2 Breaths

When providing CPR, give sets of 30 compressions and 2 breaths.

- Make sure the person is lying faceup on a firm, flat surface.
- Quickly move bulky clothes out of the way. If a person's clothes are difficult to remove, you can still provide compressions over clothing.
  - If an AED becomes available, remove all clothes that cover the chest. AED pads must not be placed over any clothing.
- Give 30 chest compressions.
  - Put the heel of one hand on the center of the chest, over the lower half of the breastbone. Put your other hand on top of the first hand.
  - Push straight down at least 2 inches.
  - Push at a rate of 100 to 120 compressions per minute. Count the compressions out loud.
  - Let the chest come back up to its normal position after each compression.
- After 30 compressions, give 2 breaths.
  - Open the airway and give 2 breaths (blow for 1 second for each). Watch for the chest to begin to rise as you give each breath.
- Try not to interrupt compressions for more than 10 seconds, even when you give breaths.

Use an AED

CPR combined with using an AED provides the best chance of saving a life. If possible, use an AED every time you provide CPR.

AEDs are safe, accurate, and easy to use. Once you turn on the AED, follow the prompts. The AED will check to see if the person needs a shock and will automatically give one or tell you when to give one.

Turn on the AED

To use an AED, turn it on by either pushing the On button or lifting the lid (Figure 62). Once you turn on the AED, you will hear prompts that tell you everything you need to do.

Figure 62. Turning on the AED.

Attach the Pads

AEDs may have adult and child pads. Make sure you use the adult pads for anyone 8 years or older. Before you place the pads, quickly scan the person to see if there are any special situations that might require additional steps (see Special Situations later in this section).

Peel away the backing from the pads. Following the pictures on the pads, attach them to the person's bare chest (Figure 63). Plug the pads connector into the AED, if necessary.

Figure 63. Place pads on an adult by following the pictures on the pads.

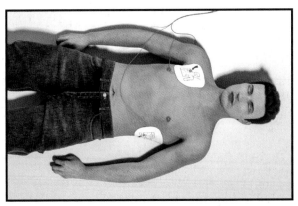

Clear the Person if a Shock Is Advised

Let the AED analyze the heart rhythm. If the AED advises a shock, it will tell you to stay clear of the person. If so, then loudly state, "Clear." Make sure that no one is touching the person just before you push the Shock button (Figure 64).

Figure 64. Make sure that no one is touching the person just before you push the Shock button.

Steps for Using an AED for an Adult

Use the AED as soon as it's available. Here are the steps for using an AED for an adult:

- Turn the AED on and follow the prompts.
  - Turn it on by pushing the On button or lifting the lid.
  - Follow the prompts that tell you everything you need to do.
- Attach the adult pads.
  - Use the adult pads for anyone 8 years or older.
  - Peel away the backing from the pads.
  - Following the pictures on the pads, attach them to the person's bare chest.
  - Plug the pads connector into the AED, if necessary.
- Let the AED analyze.
  - Loudly state, "Clear," and make sure that no one is touching the person.
  - The AED will analyze the heart rhythm.
  - If the AED tells you a shock is not needed, resume CPR.
- Deliver a shock if needed.
  - Loudly state, "Clear," and make sure that no one is touching the person.
  - Push the Shock button.
- Immediately resume CPR.

Special Situations

There are some special situations that you may need to consider before placing AED pads. Quickly scan the person to see if they have any of the following before applying the pads:

- *If the person has hair on the chest that may prevent pads from sticking, remove the hair in one of these ways:*
  - Quickly shave the area where you will place the pads by using the razor from the AED carrying case.
  - Use a second set of AED pads (if available) to remove the hair.
    - Apply the pads and press them down firmly.
    - Rip the pads off forcefully to remove the chest hair.
    - Reapply a new set of pads to the bare skin.
- *If the person is lying in water*
  - Quickly move the person to a dry area.
- *If the person is lying on snow or in a small puddle*
  - You can use the AED—the chest doesn't have to be completely dry.
  - If the chest is covered with water or sweat, quickly wipe it before attaching the pads.
- *If the person has water on the chest*
  - Quickly wipe the chest dry before attaching the pads.
- *If the person has an implanted defibrillator or pacemaker*
  - Don't put the AED pad directly over the implanted device.
  - Follow the normal steps for operating an AED.
- *If the person has a medicine patch where you need to place an AED pad*
  - Don't put the AED pad directly over a medicine patch.
  - Use protective gloves.
  - Remove the medicated patch.
  - Wipe the area clean.
  - Attach the AED pads.

- *If the person is wearing jewelry*
  - You don't need to remove a person's jewelry as long as it doesn't interfere with the placement of the pads and is not in contact with the pads. It doesn't cause a shock hazard to either the person or rescuer.
- *If the person is wearing a bra or other undergarment*
  - Bras should be removed, along with other clothes covering the chest, since they often interfere with proper pad placement.
- *If the person is pregnant*
  - Use an AED for a pregnant woman in cardiac arrest the same way you would for any cardiac arrest victim. Shock from the AED will not harm the baby.

Continue Providing CPR and Using the AED

As soon as the AED gives the shock, immediately resume chest compressions. Continue to follow the AED prompts as they guide you.

Provide CPR and use the AED until

- Someone else arrives who can take turns providing CPR with you
  - If someone else arrives, you can take turns giving compressions. Switch rescuers about every 2 minutes, which is about 5 cycles of compressions or breaths, or sooner if you get tired.
- The person begins to move, speak, blink, or otherwise react
- Someone with more advanced training arrives

Putting It All Together: Adult High-Quality CPR AED Summary

Compressions are very important to deliver blood flow. They are the core of CPR. Try not to interrupt chest compressions for more than 10 seconds when you give breaths.

Assess and Phone 9-1-1
- Make sure the scene is safe.
- Tap and shout (check for responsiveness).
  - If the person is responsive, ask, "Do you need help?"
  - If the person is unresponsive, go to the next step.
- Shout for help.
- Phone 9-1-1 and get an AED.
  - Phone or send someone else to phone 9-1-1 and get an AED.
  - If you're alone and have a cell phone or nearby phone, put it on speaker mode and phone 9-1-1.
  - If you're alone and don't have a nearby phone, leave the person while you go phone 9-1-1 and get an AED.
- Check for breathing.
  - If the person is breathing, stay with the person until advanced help arrives.
  - If the person is not breathing or is only gasping, begin CPR and use the AED. See the next steps.

Provide High-Quality CPR

When providing CPR, give sets of 30 compressions and 2 breaths.

- Make sure the person is lying faceup on a firm, flat surface.
- Quickly move bulky clothes out of the way. If a person's clothes are difficult to remove, you can still provide compressions over clothing.
  - If an AED becomes available, remove all clothes that cover the chest. AED pads must not be placed over any clothing.

- Give 30 chest compressions.
  - Put the heel of one hand on the center of the chest (over the lower half of the breastbone). Put your other hand on top of the first hand.
  - Push straight down at least 2 inches, or 5 cm.
  - Push at a rate of 100 to 120/min. Count the compressions out loud.
  - Let the chest come back up to its normal position after each compression.
- After 30 compressions, give 2 breaths.
  - Open the airway and give 2 breaths (blow for 1 second for each). As you give each breath, watch for the chest to begin to rise.
  - Try not to interrupt compressions for more than 10 seconds, even when you give breaths.
- Use an AED as soon as it is available.
  - Turn the AED on and follow the prompts.
  - Attach the adult pads.
  - Let the AED analyze.
  - Make sure that no one is touching the person, and deliver a shock if advised.
- Provide CPR and use the AED until
  - Someone else arrives who can take turns providing CPR with you
  - The person begins to move, speak, blink, or otherwise react
  - Someone with more advanced training arrives and takes over

How to Help an Adult With a Drug Overdose Emergency

Across the world, far too many people are dying from drug overdoses. These deaths are largely due to opioids. Common opioids are morphine, fentanyl, heroin, oxycodone, methadone, and hydrocodone.

Naloxone is a medication used to reverse the overdose effects of an opioid and help the person to survive. It's safe and effective. Emergency responders have used naloxone for many years.

Family members or caregivers of known opioid users may keep naloxone close by to use in case of an opioid overdose. An accidental overdose can happen to anyone. If you know someone who has access to naloxone, you may need to use it, so it's important to know how to do so.

Facts About Naloxone
- Naloxone is available without a prescription in most states and through substance use disorder treatment programs.
- Naloxone comes in several forms, including an intranasal spray or autoinjector similar to an epinephrine pen. For these forms, you'll give naloxone by spraying it into the nose or by injecting it into a muscle.
- Naloxone is used after an opioid overdose to reverse the effects. It won't work for other types of drug overdoses.

Opioid-Associated Emergency

Common signs of opioid overdose include unresponsiveness with shallow or slow breathing, or even no breathing or only gasping. You may suspect a drug overdose if you see signs of drugs nearby or if there's other evidence of drug use. If you suspect that someone has had an opioid overdose and the person is still responsive, phone 9-1-1 and stay with the person until someone with more advanced training arrives.

How to Help an Adult With an Opioid-Associated Emergency
- Make sure the scene is safe.
- Tap and shout (check for responsiveness).
- Shout for help.
- Phone or send someone else to phone 9-1-1, and get the naloxone kit and an AED. Put the phone on speaker mode.
- Check for breathing.
  - If the person is breathing normally, give the naloxone if available, and stay with the person until advanced help arrives.
  - If the person is not breathing normally or is only gasping, provide CPR, and use the AED as soon as it's available. Give the naloxone as soon as you can, but don't delay CPR to give naloxone.
- Continue giving CPR and using the AED until
  - Someone else arrives who can take turns providing CPR with you
  - The person begins to move, speak, blink, or otherwise react
  - Someone with more advanced training arrives

How to Help a Choking Adult, Child, or Infant

In this section, you will learn to assess whether someone has a mild or severe block in the airway and how to take action to help.

Overview

Choking is when food or another object gets stuck in the airway in the throat. The object can block the airway and stop air from getting to the lungs. In adults, choking is often caused by food. In children, choking can be caused by food or an object.

Topics covered in this section are

- Mild vs severe airway block
- How to help an adult, child, or infant with severe airway block
- How to help a choking adult, child, or infant who becomes unresponsive

Mild vs Severe Airway Block

The block in the airway that causes choking can be either mild or severe. A person with a **mild airway block** can talk or make sounds or can cough loudly. Stand by and let the person cough. If you're worried about the person's breathing, phone 9-1-1.

A person with a **severe airway block** cannot breathe, talk, or make sounds; has a silent cough; or makes the choking sign by holding the neck with 1 or both hands (Figure 65). When this happens, you should act quickly.

Figure 65. The choking sign: holding the neck with 1 or both hands.

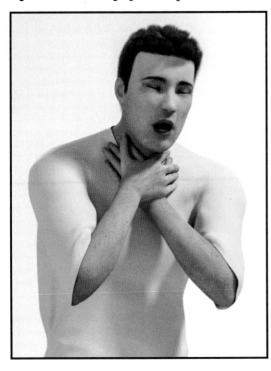

Severe Airway Block in an Adult or Child

When an adult or child has a severe airway block, give thrusts slightly above the navel. These thrusts are called *abdominal thrusts.* Like a cough, each thrust pushes air from the lungs. This can help move or remove an object that is blocking the airway.

Any person who has received abdominal thrusts should see a healthcare provider as soon as possible.

Follow these steps to help a choking adult or child with a severe airway block.

- If you think someone is choking, ask, "Are you choking? Can I help you?"
- If the person nods yes, tell them you are going to help.
- Stand firmly or kneel behind the person (depending on your size and the size of the person choking).
- Wrap your arms around the person's waist so that your fists are in front.
- Make a fist with one hand.
- Put the thumb side of your fist slightly above the person's belly button and well below the breastbone.
- Grasp the fist with your other hand and give quick upward thrusts into the abdomen (Figure 66).
- Give thrusts until the object is forced out and the person can breathe, cough, or speak, or until they become unresponsive.

Figure 66. Giving abdominal thrusts.

Severe Airway Block in a Pregnant Woman or Large Adult or Child

If the person with severe airway block is pregnant or very large, give chest thrusts instead of abdominal thrusts.

Follow these steps to help a pregnant woman or large person with a severe airway block:

- If you can't wrap your arms fully around the waist, give thrusts on the chest (chest thrusts) instead of the abdomen.
- Put your arms under the armpits and your hands on the lower half of the breastbone.
- Pull straight back to give chest thrusts (Figure 67).

Figure 67. Giving chest thrusts to a choking pregnant woman or a large adult or child.

Severe Airway Block in an Infant

When an infant has a severe airway block, use back slaps and chest thrusts to help remove the object. *Give only back slaps and chest thrusts to an infant who is choking.* Never use abdominal thrusts. Giving thrusts to an infant's abdomen can cause serious harm.

Follow these steps to help an infant with a severe airway block:

- Hold the infant facedown on your forearm. Support the infant's head and jaw with your hand.
- With the heel of your other hand, give up to 5 back slaps between the infant's shoulder blades (Figure 68A).
- If the object does not come out after 5 back slaps, turn the infant over, supporting the head.
- Give up to 5 chest thrusts, using 2 fingers of your other hand to push on the chest in the same place you push during CPR (Figure 68B).
- Repeat giving 5 back slaps and 5 chest thrusts until the infant can breathe, cough, or cry, or until they become unresponsive.

Figure 68. How to help an infant who has a severe airway block. **A,** Back slaps. **B,** Chest thrusts.

A

B

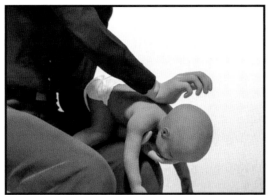 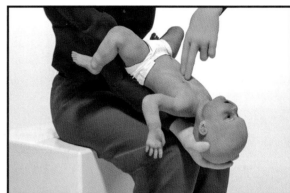

Help a Choking Adult, Child, or Infant Who Becomes Unresponsive

If you can't remove the object blocking the airway, the person will become unresponsive. Always give CPR to anyone who is unresponsive and is not breathing normally or is only gasping. Giving both compressions and breaths is very important for someone with a severe airway block who becomes unresponsive.

Remember: Unresponsive + No breathing or only gasping = Provide CPR

Choking Adult Who Becomes Unresponsive

Follow these steps to help an adult with a severe airway block who becomes unresponsive:

- Shout for help.
- Phone or have someone phone 9-1-1 and get an AED. Put the phone on speaker mode so that you can talk to the dispatcher.
- Provide CPR, starting with compressions.
- After each set of 30 compressions, open the airway to give breaths.
- Look in the mouth. If you see an object in the mouth, take it out.
- Give 2 breaths and then repeat 30 compressions.
- Continue CPR until
  - The person moves, speaks, blinks, or otherwise reacts
  - Someone with more advanced training arrives and takes over

Remember: Every time you open the airway to give breaths, look for the object in the back of the throat. If you see an object, take it out. Do not perform a blind finger sweep. This could cause the object to get lodged farther back in the airway.

Choking Child or Infant Who Becomes Unresponsive

A child or an infant who has a severe airway block and becomes unresponsive needs immediate CPR. If you are alone without a cell phone, it's important to provide 5 sets of 30 compressions and 2 breaths first. Then, you can leave the child or infant, or carry the child or infant with you, while you go to phone 9-1-1 and get an AED. Use the AED as soon as it is available.

Follow these steps to help a choking child or infant with a severe airway block who becomes unresponsive:

- Shout for help.
- Make sure the child or infant is lying faceup on a firm, flat surface.
- Begin CPR, phone 9-1-1, and get an AED. Use the AED as soon as it's available.

If someone comes to help and a cell phone is available

- Ask the person to phone 9-1-1 on the cell phone, put it on speaker mode, and go get an AED while you begin CPR.
- Use the AED as soon as it's available.

If someone comes to help and a cell phone is not available

- Ask the person to phone 9-1-1 and go get an AED while you begin CPR.
- Use the AED as soon as it's available.

If you are alone and do have a cell phone

- Phone 9-1-1 and put the phone on speaker mode while you begin CPR.
- Give 5 sets of 30 compressions and 2 breaths.
- Go get an AED, and use it as soon as it's available. (If you're alone, you can carry the child or infant with you while you go to get an AED.)
- Return to the child or infant and continue CPR.

If you are alone and don't have a cell phone

- Give 5 sets of 30 compressions and 2 breaths.
- Phone 9-1-1 and get an AED. Use the AED as soon as it's available. (If you're alone, you can carry the child or infant with you while you go to phone 9-1-1 and get an AED.)
- Return to the child or infant and continue CPR.
- Provide CPR.
  - Give sets of 30 compressions and 2 breaths.
  - After each set of 30 compressions, open the airway to give breaths.
  - Look in the mouth (Figure 69). If you see an object in the mouth, take it out. *Do not perform a blind finger sweep.*
  - Give 2 breaths.
- Continue CPR and looking in the mouth after each set of compressions until
  - The child or infant moves, cries, speaks, blinks, or otherwise reacts
  - Someone with more advanced training arrives and takes over

Figure 69. Look in the mouth for objects.

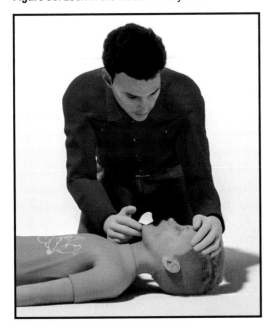

Summary of High-Quality CPR Components

Table 5 shows the components of high-quality CPR for each age group.

Table 5. Summary of High-Quality CPR Components

Component	Adult	Children (age 1 year to puberty)	Infants (age less than 1 year)
Make sure the scene is safe	Make sure the scene is safe for you and the person needing help.		
Tap and shout (check for responsiveness)	Check to see if the person is responsive or unresponsive. If unresponsive, go to the next step.		
Shout for help	Shout for help so that if others are nearby, they can help you.		
Check for breathing	If breathing normally, stay with the person until advanced help arrives. If not breathing normally or only gasping, begin CPR and use an AED.	If breathing, stay with the child or infant until advanced help arrives. If not breathing or only gasping, begin CPR and use the AED.	
Phone 9-1-1, begin CPR, and get an AED	Phone or send someone else to phone 9-1-1 and get an AED while you begin CPR. If you are alone and have a phone, put it on speaker mode and phone 9-1-1 while you begin CPR.	Phone or send someone else to phone 9-1-1 and get an AED. If you are alone and have a phone, put it on speaker mode and phone 9-1-1 while you begin CPR. If you are alone and do not have a phone, give 5 sets of 30 compressions and 2 breaths. Then, go phone 9-1-1 and get an AED. Return and continue CPR.	
Compressions and breaths	30 compressions to 2 breaths		
Compression rate	Push on the chest at a rate of 100 to 120/min		
Compression depth	At least 2 inches	At least one third the depth of the chest, or approximately 2 inches	At least one third the depth of the chest, or about 1½ inches
Hand placement	2 hands on the lower half of the breastbone	2 hands or 1 hand (optional for very small child) on the lower half of the breastbone	2 fingers or 2 thumbs in the center of the chest, just below the nipple line; 1 hand if necessary for compression depth
Let the chest come back up	Let the chest come back up to its normal position after each compression		
Minimize interruptions in compressions	Try not to interrupt compressions for more than 10 seconds, even when you give breaths		

Differences in CPR for Adults, Children, and Infants

Table 6 summarizes the differences in CPR by age group.

Table 6. Differences in CPR for Adults, Children, and Infants

Component	Adult	Children (age 1 year to puberty)	Infants (age less than 1 year)
Compression depth	At least 2 inches	At least one third the depth of the chest, or approximately 2 inches	At least one third the depth of the chest, or about 1½ inches
Hand placement	2 hands on the lower half of the breastbone	2 hands or 1 hand (optional for very small child) on the lower half of the breastbone	2 fingers or 2 thumbs in the center of the chest, just below the nipple line; 1 hand if necessary for compression depth
When to phone 9-1-1 if you are alone and without a phone	After you check breathing, before starting chest compressions	After 5 sets of 30 compressions and 2 breaths	After 5 sets of 30 compressions and 2 breaths; if the infant is uninjured, take the infant with you

Legal Questions

Good Samaritan laws exist to protect providers who help ill and injured people. The laws vary from state to state. Your instructor will talk to you about the laws that apply to you.

Duty to Provide CPR

Some people may be required to perform CPR while working. Some examples are law enforcement officers, firefighters, flight attendants, lifeguards, and park rangers. If they are off duty, they can choose whether or not to provide CPR.

Providing CPR may be part of your job description. If so, you must help while you're working. However, when you're off duty, you can choose whether to provide CPR.

After the Emergency

If you provide CPR, you may learn private things about a person. You must not share this information with other people. Keep private things private.

Remember to

- Give all information about the person to EMS rescuers or the person's healthcare providers
- Protect the person's privacy

Conclusion

Congratulations on completing this Heartsaver course!

Practice your skills. Review the steps in this workbook often. This will keep you prepared to give first aid care and high-quality CPR whenever it's needed. Even if you don't remember all the steps exactly, it's important for you to try. Any help, even if it isn't perfect, is better than no help at all. And remember to phone 9-1-1 when an emergency arises. The dispatcher will remind you what to do.

Contact the AHA if you want more information on CPR, AEDs, or first aid. You can visit **cpr.heart.org** or call 1-877-AHA-4CPR (877-242-4277) to find a class near you.